Heaven

MANUEL VILAS is a Spanish writer, the author of several books, including fourteen collections of poetry, seven books of essays, and seven novels. His most recent novel, *Alegría*, was the 2019 Premio Planeta Finalista, and its predecessor, *Ordesa*, was a bestseller in Spain, won the French Prix Femina Étranger in 2019, and is forthcoming in a number of languages, including French, German and English. Vilas currently divides his time between Spain and the United States, where he teaches at the University of Iowa.

JAMES WOMACK was born in Cambridge in 1979. He studied Russian, English and translation at university, and received his doctorate, on W.H. Auden's translations, in 2006. After ten years in Madrid, he has recently returned to the UK, where he teaches Spanish and translation at Cambridge University. He is a freelance translator from Russian and Spanish, and helps run Calque Press, which concentrates on poetry, translation and the environment. His debut collection of poems, *Misprint*, was published by Carcanet in 2012, and *On Trust: A Book of Lies* came out in December 2017. A third collection, *Homunculus*, is due out in August 2020.

T0287518

MANUEL VILAS

Heaven

Translated by James Womack

CARCANET

Acknowledgements

The translator expresses his sincere gratitude to Manuel Vilas for his continued support and encouragement in the preparation of these translations. Thanks also to *PN Review*, which awarded the translation of 'Macbeth' its inaugural Translation Prize, and where versions of some of these poems have previously appeared. The first draft of this book was completed during a fellowship at Hawthornden Castle in April 2019: thanks to the Hawthornden Foundation for its trust.

First published in Great Britain in 2020 by
Carcanet Press Ltd
Alliance House, 30 Cross Street
Manchester M2 7AQ
www.carcanet.co.uk

Text copyright © Manuel Vilas and James Womack, 2020

A CIP catalogue record for this book is available from the British Library.
ISBN 978 1 784108 86 1

The publisher acknowledges financial assistance from Arts Council England.

Typeset in England by XL Publishing Services, Exmouth
Printed and bound in England by SRP Ltd, Exeter

Contents

HEAVEN (2000)

Rosaries and Flick-Knives

Story of a Chambermaid

The Swimmer

Heat (2008)

HEAVEN

(2000)

*Tus ojos me recuerdan
las noches de verano.*
A. Machado

Rosaries and Flick-Knives

A Hundred Years Later

(Madrid, June '98)

No, you look, look at all the life here, look as much as you want.
Look at the cities filled with slaves, with wretched men.
I am just a student of philosophy
about to do the state exam, who spends his summer reading,
slowly, all of your books.
I never went to Germany, although I did learn Greek –
but I forgot it; I forgot it because I had to find a way
to earn a living: now it is thinking that supports me.
And I am here, in a room,
facing your thousands of words, words that no one believes in,
ruined words, words that will help me, if I remember them well,
to win a spot as a teacher in a provincial school
somewhere in Spain, in a country that you – I'm sure you had your
    reasons –
that you did not care to visit, to know, to travel across, to put your
    finger into.
No, believe me, there are no Spanish geniuses
in this philosophy textbook.

I was in your country once, years ago, on a package tour:
my whole life has been done on the cheap, but I loved it like you
    said
we should love all that flows from us
in a constant exhalation; and I was not fooled,
and rejected all vice, all drugs, the sandals the slave wears.

The world, the world you fell in love with, is over:
nature is a ruined old dame, melancholic,
stinking and unpleasant;
the mountains threw out their guardian angels, who died;
life itself lost the will to live, and is sick,
bedridden in a nursing home.

A hundred years have gone by and you have not returned, you will
    never return;

you fucked up there, but knew you would fuck up: like a leisure-class
anarchist, like a raving bourgeois who inhales
a new, pagan and seditious immortality.

And tell me if that is not in itself the drama: you left
and have no reason to live again, trapped in the lie that is death;
how clumsy our desires are, and our thoughts, and our theories,
and the hours we spent on the hard thought that leads
to a single enormous utopia; and time went by, and your life went
    by as well.

And my life goes by, less stressed than yours, which is why I am
    here, today,
moaning about it. The Greeks came to you, the arrogant-in-will,
the death of God... and women, all of them in love with your cruel
    talent,
and you felt them up with the rough hand of Dionysus;
and then there was the pure disdain for everything that came
    before you,
everything derived from the most perfect minds of the past;
but what about me? What is left for me
apart from your work in paperback editions, with underlinings
where I thought I found something important: ideas that,
    tomorrow –
if I am lucky and they ask me about you
rather than about Aristotle, or Aquinas, or even poor old Kant –
I'll have to explain as though I were hard-working, prudent,
    honourable?

Rosaries, Flick-Knives

I took a trip to Lourdes in France, in July '98;
that radiant time, days of cold beer and wretched lovers
on the Paris highway.
                    There are no casinos in Lourdes,
but there are a hundred hotels for the pilgrims who come to pray
    and beg,
like me, for a long life, bullish health, and for the Virgin
to make a mistake and allow the irreverent sinner
the cure of his soul, or his body, or of both at once,
together in their platonic marriage.

Lourdes is the mall of every temple, the place
where they sell rosaries, flick-knives, unhappy souvenirs,
blue virgins, two-way mirrors which pretend to show
the incarnation of the Holy Ghost – in classic bad taste
and with a mysticism proper to a Spanish raffle –
cloaks, prayers, speeches, holy water and the whole range
of famous *La main couronnée*-brand knives,
as well as a horrible Tour de France bumper sticker.

Your hand can brandish a rosary or a flick-knife.
I saw many priests in soutanes, young priests, handsome ones,
African priests, now very numerous: this black priest,
with his thick-framed glasses, full of hope, his lips set hard
as Christ's own martyrological gaze;
black priests in the service of the white invader's religious frenzy.
Black priests have always restored my faith in Rome.

Tal vez haya hoy un milagro, someone said, in the Spanish
of Latin America, that miracle-saturated, ragged land.
And at seven on the dot the procession of wheelchairs:
Canadians, English, Italians, French, Poles, Russians;
a whole rich, thoughtful and crippled world, searching here
for the last fount of hope and fantasy.
Baseless hope is the true structure of our lives.

I ate in a McDonald's, because there is a McDonald's in Lourdes:
a goodly burger and chips, and a glass
of Coke with ice, thirty-five
francs the lot; I ate alongside nuns, postulants, novices and believers.
I, a man alone, one hand on my hamburger,
the other holding a large yellow chip, thin-cut and rather overcooked;
an absurd tourist, a guy who travels
to the moral limits of this great white world: your hand can brandish
a rosary or a flick-knife, or perhaps both at the same time.

In my hotel room, with its view of the river of greenish water
that smells of incense – everything in Lourdes smells of incense,
of cruellest illness, of conservative romanticism,
of the nineteenth century, of the works of Chateaubriand,
of sacristies with their golden shadows,
of sin and ecstasy,
of plus-size girdles designed specifically for nuns,
of sackcloth bras for the novices,
of sweaty cassocks, of friars' sandals,
of omelettes and boiled cod,
of beds which when their sheets are turned back smell of death,
of all souls, of all saints –
in my hotel room I lay on my damp bed all that I bought in those
    shops
that look so much like those of the Costa Dorada:
a cheap and jazzy rosary, and a *La main couronnée* flick-knife,
the pride of the collection, the showiest,
the longest, the widest, the most expensive,
on which I have spent my last two hundred francs.

They say that the one who has been cheated draws all his misfortune
from a single, worn-out and repetitive archetype, a single face;
his own face, I would say, seen over time,
the nightmare of being alive, the happy nightmare of a much-loved
    life.
I hope it makes me suffer so much that it turns into God Itself.

I open the balcony in the Hotel Bernadette:
a white balcony whose shutters seem to presuppose a farewell ballad,

and I recall everything I have been and I don't know where I'll
    travel tomorrow,
when this August night is the equal of my desire and my prayers,
because I too am dying out – I know all too well I am dying out –
but this voluptuousness, unhealthy, average, exhausted, monastic,
which sucks the air and the holiness from all that burns and is alive,
and this city which postulates and sleeps on its knees,
and this Machiavellian essence of Christianity and all the idols,
this liturgy of flick-knives and rosaries which will die with me,
and this whisky which I drink almost madly as the dawn brightens,
and these blows to the heart:
they all tell me that my sins,
my underhand behaviour, my petty avarice and my stubborn
    sacrilege,
the idol which dwelt in me and which vanished like a self-
    acknowledged traitor,
the pain, my pain, my old suffering, so tired and so separate,
these days, these years, this moving from village to village, alone,
    dreaming –
old man in a threadbare robe where the world's flowers
hang so wretchedly,
and sometimes not so wretchedly but rather divinely or at least
    happily –
all these years travelling through Aragon, wearing Ivan the
    Terrible's face,
all of this time has at last turned good, pure and noble,
or majestic and innocent, very beautiful, very cold, very much like
    Ulysses
tempted by the sirens with their round buttocks and black
    mouths...
And with the consciousness of a man who has drunk
too much for an evening alone by himself, I fall onto my bed,
naked as a bride on her wedding night.
And it is in fact July, in what is still the greatest summer of my life.

Macbeth

This morning I got on the ferry that runs to La Gomera
from Santa Cruz de Tenerife; I sat at the deck
bar and started on the Campari and the olives,
and after a while I was completely hammered; a Scottish woman
 – scruffy and heavily made-up, around 40, fat inches of cleavage,
showing off her beautiful dark balanced breasts –
sat down to drink with me; she studied Spanish
at Madrid University, she said, and stuck out her tongue
as she did so; 'Where is Scotland?' I asked,
to which she replied, 'And where's your cock?'
And we switched from Campari to gin,
and after a while I spoke to this Scottish woman:
an inspired screed in Spanish, which she did not understand at all:

Blessed is everything that lies beneath the water,
from the shipwreck to the rhinestone necklace
that fell into the sea in an act of loving carelessness.

The book of my life lies also beneath the waves,
kept there by some rusty enchantment;
there, with the fish and coral, the seaweed and darkness.

The Scot laughed and took off her shorts
and was left wearing just her pants as though they were
a bikini, come on, take off your pants I said, let's leave the deck,
take them off, and she took them off, and in a corner of the boat,
in a little room full of overalls and an empty
bucket, we screwed like two drunks without scruples,
but with the good fortune and skill to get stuck into one another,
and afterwards, I took her earrings and threw them in the sea,
and she took my wallet and said you're a sad sack of shit,
those earrings were made of gold and worth ten dicks like yours,
and she took from my wallet the ten banknotes I'd been keeping
to be able to eat alone on the island, drink gin in some bar on the
    beach.

The kingdom of God is decorated with the gold
all the best men have brought Him,
I smoked a lot that night and was coughing; I went from dive
to dive, and at dawn there was only warm beer left;
you look like a renegade saint, or else a beggar, one of my listeners said.

Distant and shrivelled, all heroes abandoned the heaven and the earth:
their distance makes my life sad; their neglect is my abandonment.
I grew up with them, a child waiting at a balcony over a river,
or swimming in the sea on July evenings,
and I heard them come and they did not come.
I heard them speak to me and they did not speak;
I heard them love me, and they forgot about me.

The sea takes my vulgar gift, those gold earrings,
in honour of the centuries that it has been alone,
and is pleased that I remembered about her for once.
Life has rotted away,
I cannot always be in love,
and now I desire nothing.

The night filled with stars, the white whale,
the tenth century BC, a hut plonked in the middle of the world,
a river, a language with no way of being set down, fruits,
vegetables, a couple of goats, a wounded hare, a fire,
a cave, a lambskin, a stone-tipped spear;
the sea like a shield, like the bare flesh of every sin,
and the gods, petty, invented,
the forest, snow, the fire; the sea is pure terror,
gross terror, the faces of the dead, death itself,
the dolmen, the granite,
the sense that God is coming.

Black lens of the ocean, crypt of salt water far below me,
the photograph of a distant past; there was nothing,
and nothing wishes to dwell in me,
and the sea pulls back and the dawn comes
and I go back to the hotel where I am staying.
The child vanished; the heroes sang and were never heard,

the sea strode on to a great silence,
and I got drunk
and spent the whole afternoon asleep.

And I should expect nothing from all the gifts that accompany old age,
such as honour, and love, and tact and obedience,
and the whole grand army of my friends.

Storm in the Air

For ten years now I have slept by day and by night.
I have come to the coast to try to wake up. I was left alone;
my wife left me for another woman, and I knew nothing until it
    happened;
I was left with my dog Trajan, another sleeping beauty;
as for my uncle's inheritance, I spent uncle Valero's money
on hookers: Valencian, Catalan,
Andalucian, Basque and African, and then I started on the French,
the Chinese, the Peruvian;
and I started to travel, like a storm travels,
throwing off water and black clouds, rain and hail,
destroying harvests
and soaking the lovers who sit kissing in parks or suburban streets.

I lived here and there, spent time in cities like Rome or Paris,
alone, rich, rich enough, a man of leisure, enjoying my inheritance,
looking at houses, bars, men,
restaurants and shops.
With money and no job, and beautiful Paris streets before me.
Serious sins, little white sins, alleyways, the banks of the Seine,
theatres, poison, all the drinks I've already drunk, Gabriela's light –
she was a lover I had, her old flat, an exorcism, a miracle,
the moon above us, the vast storm that was unleashed that summer;
Gabriela who spoke about her father, an Argentine who died
in Germany, crushed by a train, a ghost who came to her,
a meticulous werewolf, Nietzschean, the horror and frenzy of life.

I have been the most innocent, the best travelled, the quietest.
I used to take photos of the hotel rooms where I slept:
the bed, the desk, the window, the rug, the shower...
and then I stopped: I had so many photos that I didn't know
where to keep them – a strongbox in the Swiss Embassy, perhaps.
I asked for a key to my room, 224, and a concierge treated me with
great ceremony; I went up in the lift, opened the door
and was alone: I put on the TV and spent the night watching
French TV, deeply alone,

and then a TV movie, and then a proper film, *The Accidental Tourist*.
No one knew where I was; by now nobody knew me at all.

Once I fell in love with a woman I had barely seen
at the next table in the restaurant, a woman wearing white,
about thirty years old, thirty-five perhaps; at other times
I sought refuge in museums, and spent whole hours
in front of paintings by Delacroix, or else went to graveyards
where last century's poets were buried,
and I always went alone, always wishing to be more alone, dreaming
of a harder loneliness, a greater loneliness,
and an impossible perfection.

Men were ungrateful to me,
and I guess women were as well.

The Last Man

Vuestra Merced escriba se le escriba
Lazarillo

Sitting on a summer terrace in Mallorca,
I said to a friend, the inspiration of a gin and tonic inside me:
'That children can go hungry is the only important thing
in history, in society, in all philosophy.
The guillotines of the future will be erected by the hungry.
God is the idol of the poor.'

I don't know why I think these things or write about them,
ideas that are so banal, the kind of thing a village curate
would come up with, one who had never seen the cities of Europe
and their trainee nuns,
the kind of nuns who get made up and go out at night,
with their new, never-been-kissed lips and hard bodies,
twenty years old and their pants already wet.

I took another swig of my gin and knew that I was alone,
in Mallorca, in a church square filled with grockles:
I patted my wallet, chewed on my glasses, patted Trajan,
and carried on: 'If we had any shame at all we would be missionaries,
you and I, Trajan, you would carry a Red Cross first aid kit
on your wonderful back.
I am a witty curate, a wolf singled out in the darkness;
I am a desert preacher, grown deaf;
I am a retired theologian, an enlightened shaman,
a holy matchmaker, a half-blind guide,
a seashell that has been elevated to heaven,
an inspired being who burns only for himself,
a party with a single guest,
bored, geometrical, lunar;
I am the son of God, the last one he had.
I will not dedicate my life to the service of truth.
I was born in July '72, I am a child of summer,
of Spanish summer, summer of sun and parties at night,
parties for the body, for the mouth, for the feet,

for the older women's ass, for the thighs
of the hired woman where a tattoo burns;
the tattoo is of an open mouth, and the summer is dying of hunger.
July, Spain, thirst, the modern thirst to do nothing
except take the sun, get naked, be naked,
dick like a concrete pole, drinking beer and wine all day.
July, Spain, the rich incompetent and lazy,
and the poor both poor and sad.'

Story of a Chambermaid

Insomniac Whims

At night, when I can't sleep for being so happy,
I get out of bed and listen to music and write,
and leaf vaguely through the papers that come from the bank;
I check the clocks in my house: my house is full
of clocks; I iron a shirt or two if the spirit moves me;
I look at the domestic slumber of Trajan the Great and tidy
the desk in my office, shine my shoes and write
without much self-belief, and remember all my childhood friends
and think of a cliff by the sea's edge, and in the sea a boat
full of my little friends, all sailing like champions.

On my office desk are: the photos of Kafka
(I told my cleaner that he was my great-grandfather
and she said he was very handsome, and that I had his eyes);
a screwdriver that I got in the sales, and which I now use
to kill the transparent fair-weather insects that sneak into
the house in search of my desk lamp; a calculator
made by Firstline, that I use for my life's sad, cheap sums;
a rubber stamp with my name and address; a stapler –
black with gold trim, very pretty; the glasses
for my discreet myopia; the sunglasses that should not
be here, and a diary filled with useless addresses and numbers.

And in the desk drawer I have a beautiful knife that I use, every
now and then, to threaten, with playful extravagance, Trajan the
      Great,
who tells me off with an angry melodramatic bark or two.
By night, as long as my vigil lasts, I go through the nooks and crannies
of my house, in the dark; I pick up the telephone and hear the voice
in the answering machine as it tells me I have no messages,
no new messages and nothing saved; I'm scared to open the
      wardrobes;
I like to touch the cold handles of all the doors
in my house, and then, after this nocturnal round,
I go back to my bed, take my slippers off, plump the pillow,
and as I try to fall asleep say an Ave Maria, a Credo and a Pater
      Noster.

And there is still time for a single blue tear to slide
over my clasped hands, over my bared chest, over my damp cheek.

Summer is the season when I fell in love with you
and knew what life could bring; we went down to the river together,
and Spain was a dictatorship collapsing on top of us.
And all I know to say (like one of those creatures obsessed by his
    few words
that barely represent the facts) is *summer is the season
when I fell in love with you*, and I could only at a pinch add, 'Know
    this'.
But – 'know this'? – isn't that 'know this' a sign of arrogant rhetoric,
as no one ever knew anything about us, and no one will know how
    I loved you,
because lovers like us leave no traces, leave nothing at all.

The Last Swimmers

These children are now become the last swimmers
of the August afternoon.
                          Parents' voices call them back
with a false severity. The last swimmers
want to enjoy the water just one more time,
in endless jubilation.

The August twilight loves these prepubescent swimmers,
the essence of summer, noble ragamuffins of fine weather
and innocent joy.
Swim on, jump,
keep on with your acrobatics,
until the sun no longer warms
the water and you are proud and cold.

One of them, the last swimmer, looks at me
with his throne open for business, holding time in one hand.
Oh, serenity, grant this kid what you granted
every foolish man: zeal and few questions,
zeal and a rich body,
floating on a sketch drawn from life.

Thirty-Six Years Old

Stairs wear me out, it's hard to write, it's hard to sleep,
everything that inspired me in the past now seems a load of rubbish;
I like money, the Christmas holidays, public holidays, snow, sun;
there's not much difference between me and good old Trajan, we
    grew up
together, and I have seen the spiritual essence of man's life
dragging itself like an old cripple down the street
in hope's very own Chinatown; I will start to turn into
an animal with no idols, no gods, no church, no brothers,
like Trajan himself, who with every day is happier, more truly a dog.

The whole of life steps forward one morning at the end of July.
I am reading a book and at my side there's a glass
of white wine, yesterday's newspaper on the table,
and I'm listening to Lou Reed who is singing something like
what I am writing. My joints ache:
it must be the bloody mattress that is getting old and that I
should change: Jesus, how much is a new mattress?
My back hurts, my eyes, my left foot;
when I tell my mother I'm a bitter old man she gets scared;
when I tell one of my made-up friends –
like Florencio, who appears in some of my novels –
that I'm a shrivelled old mummy, he says no, I'm just on edge,
it's my imagination, my thought getting hard payback
from my body. How discreet middle age is, how false
the indications time gives us, how vain is human blood.
What a hypocrite I am, I who am not even old.

I'm going to have a shower right now, shave, brush my hair,
go out into the street clean and in fresh clothes, brand new trousers,
brand new shoes and a shirt, I'll try to be happy all night long
as I go from bar to bar, chatting to the anonymous boys and girls
– I too am anonymous, a Black man, a Chinese, a dried-out Gypsy – ;
and I will pray and drink simultaneously, and at dawn, if I have not
    found
a loose (very loose) Filipina woman to love me, I will go home,
filled with fame and death, filled with light.

Let the Lord God number me among the saints; I have just
turned thirty-six; I like films about guns and aliens,
I like ten-thousand peseta notes, I like doing nothing,
I like to pray for the life I have led
And for the days to come, the New Year's Eves, the birthdays,
holidays by the sea and retirement and a cheap headstone;
I like expensive cars, the folk art
of Pedro Páramo; I like women – black women, white women;
I like trees, olives, trips to Cuba,
famous restaurants, high boots that squeak when you walk,
sharp knives, mountains, all the sad oceans and the moon.
Someone who has lived a little and been around,
will say, like in a good film, 'Fuck you, spic',
and my hand will be steady as I put a bullet in his throat.

Brandeso-Station

Is it true that the saints cry out through the thunder?
That's how it seemed to me, one August afternoon,
in the Pyrenean village of Brandeso-Station.
The whole atmosphere was muggy and delirious,
filled with wild gestures and tragic inhalations,
just as I was, ten years ago, and the hand of God
covered the mountain peaks –
where the eagles
the dead and the lovers all dance –
hiding them from our sight.

So many clouds, spread out like violent sails,
came to us from the hungry lands,
though all is hungry in the kingdom of the sky,
and turned my roof into an accordion of ash.
The little tarn, Ibón de Estanés, felt water fall on its water,
and night, that perverse mountain night, the unwelcoming
night of God among his mountains, broke with truth.

My hand is frozen and my mind is frozen in mid-
August, frozen flesh of the tarns, black smoke.

The tourists gave up on their harmless excursions,
and hid in the open bars and cafes.
The cars did not stop at the souvenir shops;
the cyclists protected themselves with sporty raincoats.
'It's August, just an August storm,' an elderly gentleman said,
sitting next to me, reading the newspaper.

'It's Brandeso-Station,' I said,
'one out of all the cold kingdoms.'

Summer Night

How much have I changed over these last few years,
and how happy I am to have changed so much;
how I love all the great cities of the earth,
and how little I care that everything dies,
how little I care that the stars enter their final agony;
how much have I changed from who I was, and how happy I am
to know how I used to be, how I loved
and lived; how happy I am that beautiful women kiss me,
that they freely touch my body just as I touch theirs;
how happy I am that I read Catullus when I was fourteen,
and Rubén Darío when I was sixteen; how beautiful are the beaches
where I slept as a young man, how sweet was that teenager,
the first girl I kissed; all will go to the kingdom of God
and I will have my fun again there, and if not, well, how little
it will matter to me, because that's what life was for:
life was a secret, a great joy, life itself is
much more than we allow life to be, so much more,
but I should have realised, I should have known that well enough.
It was too large, and still is; too perfect,
that's what life is: money beyond reckoning, huge estates, vast
holdings in America, in Asia, in Paris, Rome, Berlin,
new flats and old flats in the city centre, all mod cons,
jewels, paintings, classic cars, horses,
houses and castles all over the shop, fortune after fortune
amassed throughout history; it hurts that life is
so enormous, it hurts that life is so intelligent.
All life is our hospital, the forsaken word.
This is how I enjoy my dreams, my food and the air,
my travels and the beach, the tree, the knife
I will plunge into my heart, the streets,
the beggars, the patios where clothes flutter
on their lines, the fireworks
celebrating the local festival of some shit-hole village,
festival of a river that doesn't even cover your ankles
and where you have to fight with the rocks in order
to bathe at all, festival of a lorry abandoned in the middle of the
    road

with all its tyres slashed and its windows broken,
and inside which I would like to make love to myself.
I adore my past; I adore what I once was;
I know all too well what I once was,
I know the causes that made me what I was, and I adore them,
and I adore what I shall be tomorrow
and I will adore myself throughout eternity,
while it is possible for a man to adore this oh-so-adorable life.

Insomniac Memories

How perfect you were in the dawn light lying on the sofa
in my room, naked, smoking, reading a magazine;
your lips red, smiling like you were extremely wealthy:
I inherited a lot of money from my Swiss uncle, you said at dinner.

A woman who travels the world, lover of beaches and good
    weather,
made of light, terrifyingly young; *you will never grow old*
I said to you, and you: *kiss me here, on my hands, among the rubies.*
I shall, I replied, *isn't this suite big, how beautiful the sea*
when the dawn comes in. I like the South, although everything bores me,
and we did it once again, standing by the window, with our hands
on the windowsill, me taking her from behind, *How old are you?*
You'd like me to say eighteen, but I'm past thirty.
The music was the *Cabaret* soundtrack, and it was already hot.

Then, still naked, you looked at yourself in the suite's horrible mirror
and said, *come here, come close, choose a part of my body,*
whichever you want; pass me a cigarette, call room
service, call the airport, I want to go to Paris.
And I: *It's better to go to Stockholm, or Helsinki, somewhere cold,*
far away from this impatient summer, and you: *come here, choose a part*
of my body, anywhere, choose anywhere in the world, kiss me slowly.
I once killed a man; I could kill you too.
And I: *I've always wanted to be killed by a woman like you, I've lived*
long enough; do it now, I won't move a muscle,
I promise; plan it while I take a shower; plan your perfect crime.

And she kissed me again. *No, you kill me; I've had a lot of love;*
kill me with your hands, I need nothing from you,
but I could be your slave, you are so beautiful sometimes –
that lip, that hand, that noble gesture, that hard soul,
this silence: it all makes you covetable. You covet from me
the same as I do from you, the secret of what we were, and this secret
made us love each other tonight; go now; I hope we never meet again.
Yes, I really hope so, let me look at you again; I cannot touch you,
I am ruined; I could fuck another man right now,

you get me? Life gave us an inexhaustible nature:
go now; I want to sleep for a while and forget about you.

Imagine that just you and I were left on this planet,
and that we were back in the year 1,000 B.C.,
and that there were no roads or cities or states or governments,
but rather caves and villages, wooden houses by the river, and a
    vast moon
on summer nights; think about that while you sleep.

A Poor Man's Biarritz

From Brandeso-Station, one July morning,
I travelled to Biarritz; I stopped in Oloron Sainte-Marie,
a French village with a river running through it,
the river where Heraclitus would have wanted to drown and vanish,
a bottomless river, with no stones, only a current,
a constant green soft flowing, lustrous and feminine.
It was nine a.m. and France was naked,
and I was crazy happy, high as a white cloud.

I went to the beaches at Biarritz; I bathed and fought
against the waves, and I was alone in that crowd.
I left my hands in the waves, and my false consciousness.
The restaurants were very expensive; the hotels served no one
but businessmen, film stars and highly successful novelists.
I took a slash at the corner of Le Pays Basque Hotel,
and as I had a semi-rection, the doorman, who was an Arab,
a Catalan and a rent boy, all three things at once,
gave me a smile that was both anarchic and hypocritical.
I drank cold beer, and spent my money on white gin,
and I looked at the sea, went back to the water, went down, dived
with no air and sank my fist into the sand underwater;
I wanted to be down there, and out at sea,
fainting, drunk, tired to have swum so much.
I went out to the city, wet and sad and in love with nothing.
I went through streets and bars, shops and promenades.
In love with nobody, damp, suddenly sober.
The light was arrogant, like a diva in the sky.
The light was a black German woman, tired of fucking so many men.
And the sky tore out my heart, tore the calm out of my life.
And so I went back to the sea, I fell down on the hard wet sand,
and I looked at the sun, the sun and the sunshades,
the naked women, the naked teenagers,
the surfers made desperate by the afternoon's tiny waves,
and I was alone in that golden crowd
of French bodies, generation upon generation,
fathers and sons, and young grandmothers, in their simple flesh.

For the love of God, why am I so happy if all I have
is death riding my back and this fistful of coins for my salary?

It is the midday sun that strips me of my conscience,
makes me into a creature of good weather and the sea,
in this Biarritz where the nineteenth century is still present
among all the tourists and their colours and their casinos,
among the young swimmers who leap from the gentle slopes,
among the flourishing businessmen, the brilliant sportsmen,
the pedigree dogs on the bustling terraces.

I went up and down streets: modern buildings, rich men's houses
with their gardens and tennis courts, snooty hotels, the Mercedes
filled with half-naked teenage girls, showing off their graceful
    bodies,
and I was poor with nowhere to stay, until I entered the courtyard
of a house up for sale, scuffed paint and dirt,
and there, death and time both said: 'You are ours now'.
The light, made of flesh, embraced my own flesh; my hand trembled,
and the sea was inside me, the flesh of the sea.
The smell of the sea's flesh stunned me, and I fell,
and I went into its terror and its past, the sea's past,
its vast history, its history of flesh, of its whole body, how glorious
is the sea's body, its confused flesh, its great thirst,
its millennia of solitude, its glaciations, the centuries in their
    millions;
learn this solitude, go and return, always alone, go and return,
and there was never anything, nothing, nothing happened, this go
    and return
of flesh, the smell, the salt, the salt scurf, the wind,
there is nothing, there was nothing, an unknowing blanket of water.
My skin burned, and I swam, and it was summer, cunning summer.

No, I am no more than the midday sun, the sea and the heat,
July heat, August heat, high season heat: such high seasons
of the body and the conquest of cold: that's where I come from.
I left the courtyard, went back to the sand and fell asleep.
I am a creature of the fine weather, a wandering bather,
an ancient swimmer, a museum piece,

I said, again and again, in my baroque and sonorous Spanish
down at the police station, where they took me
like a beggar in my bathing costume,
with a *La main couronnée*-brand flick-knife in my pocket.

I bought the knife in Lourdes, *mon ami*, I said to the young inspector.
I have only come here to take the sun and bathe in the sea.
I have only come here to play in the sand
with your girlfriend and all her friends, and your mother, and your
    sister.

Story of a Chambermaid

I am on top of the covers, sleepless, dawn is breaking in Cádiz,
the seagulls bring the new day, which I don't know if I'll make it
     through,
because I want to die, and there's a knock at the door and it's room
service, which has brought me a delicious breakfast: I try
a little bit of everything, and I went out naked to get my tray,
and the twenty-ish chambermaid blushed, *it is ze beach and ze sea*,
I said in a French accent, pretending to be a tourist,
and she so pretty in her blue housecoat, and so clean and so cute,
and you could see how well she had slept last night; come on, come
     in,
I said, show me what colour your panties are and I'll give you a
     fistful
of dollars, I just want to know what colour they are and maybe see
if they're a little old, a little worn, how much do they pay you,
     show me
and I'll give you my wallet and you can take whatever you want.
The coffee is good, the croissant has honey on it and the fruit is
ripe, and she put one foot up on the chair and lifted her
skirt and she wasn't wearing panties, she showed me her ass,
her beautiful maid's ass and she laughed a good long while,
and I was tempted to touch her ass but why bother,
why should you stroke a wild animal like this one, that hides
in the guise of an innocent chambermaid, just to see
this whim of hers, her pantylessness, her virginal cheek,
her sweet flesh, her firm thigh, her smooth well-ordered hair, this
     is enough,
and I gave her a cheque for a hundred big ones because I thought
that I would die that morning, but the surprise of finding my maid
not wearing pants, not black pants or red or white pants, has given
     me
back my lust for life, because life is an endless fantasy.
I say goodbye and then I say what the ghost of Hamlet's
father says to his son – *remember me* – in a deep theatre voice,
and she smiles at me, and goes off contented with her small fortune.
And I am happy again, and leave the *café au lait* and the toast
and pour some gin into the orange juice glass, and it is already hot,

and I look at the sea from my balcony, and I shave
and I shower, and I walk naked through the room, and I drink
 some more,
and I put on my beautiful summer suit and go out into the street.

Costa Dorada

I remember the French and German women naked on the sand:
those firm asses, gym-toned, their short blonde hair,
their shaven crotches, their bastard husbands out on rented
pedalos, their daughters moving their precious breasts through the
    air,
and the guy in charge of renting the pedalos with a hard-on
for the mothers and the daughters. 'These sluts need more than
just one man, that's what they say, so you wait till they call you,
and if they don't call you I'd just lie down here
and show off the munificent packet that I got from my dear old
    mother.'

What do you have against God, against life, against happiness,
against the body, against pleasure, against beauty?

Now I remember July, the young summer that promised
a season without weapons, the wide-open midday, the surrendering
    moon.

Men have time and they have thought;
the mountains, the trees and the sea have nothing.

I remember the young redhead, both of us curled on a single towel,
by the night sea, making love like professionals on a sound set.
And then the hotel pool, the shower, the chicken and chips.
On the bedside table a novel by Bernhard, that Austrian who hated
Austria; lots of whisky, lots of cold beer,
and I remember a weekend in Paris, *fucking expensive*
as you said on the plane, in a July about
ten years ago, drunk, naked in the hotel corridor begging for
a fresh-baked croissant for my avid and demanding lover,
who was in the shower, taking a piss for fun in the bidet,
and there is no metaphor here, but realism (either Stendhal
or Galdós): feet with red-painted nails, ass planted on the porcelain,
legs wide open and the noise of water flowing.

I do not forget the works of God but rather I observe them
from out of my temptation and my pleasure, my promiscuity and
    nightmare,
from my instinct and the flower of sainthood,
from violence, from out of holy violence.
From the extravagance that comes with the years and the
    minimum wage.

Two young people, on a park bench, next to the beach,
bid farewell to August by making love in an old-fashioned filmic
    way.
Anyone can see them, and this just throws more muck onto their
    lust,
anyone can see the boy's ass, see how he pulls
his jeans down with his legs, sunk deep
between his girlfriend's legs, the small breasts
of a twenty-year-old with a tattoo round one nipple,
the defiant freedom with which they fuck,
this freedom to fuck, to bite, to screw without any promises:
twenty years old, I was in love with myself too back then.

Man in Love

All night dreaming of you, I spent the whole night
dreaming that I was kissing you in a church square by the sea.
I was so deeply in love with you and I never told you.
Did you guess? Did you want me to be in love? Did you beg for my
    love?
You were six years older than I was, more secure in your life,
you didn't lose your head like I did, but were moderate and prudent,
although you were filled with love, love for me,
for me, a loser of the most obvious sort, and yes
that was something you saw straight out, and I remember your hands
and your smile, all lovers remember the same things,
except I was never in your bed, I've spent years imagining
what it must be like in your bed, and one day you showed me
but nothing else. Now I wake up and I dreamt I was kissing you,
and it is ten a.m. in some monumental summer
and I am already drinking gin, on an empty stomach, and I go
out onto the balcony of my room and see the tourists collapse
on the sand, and I think you could be there with me,
and how in love with you I was, how in love with me you were,
and how wrong we went when we didn't fall together
into a thousand beds, or how right, because, knowing me,
I might have asked you to marry me and you might have said yes,
and as I'm drunk all day, once I had grown tired
of fucking you every night I might well have punched you
or thrown you into a river, and you might have shot me,
or poisoned me, or fucked someone else.
How can I say all this about you, who are an angel
and will always be one, and about me, who loved you in all innocence.
It would be better for me to drink until I wipe you from my mind,
and that thought does make me cry, and so I am a man who cries
at ten thirty a.m. on the balcony of a hotel room,
a tourist hotel room, with a warm gin in his hand – all that remains
from the night – a man who cries because, if I forget you,
then yes, indeed, absolutely, there will be nothing left for me.

The Swimmer

Trainee Vampire

(La Caleta, Cádiz)

I don't remember anything now and I am happily alone.
I like to walk along the beach with an ice cream in my hand, a
    Magnum,
a white chocolate Magnum, and sometimes I think I'm a kind
    vampire,
unworthy of the moral rigour of the underworld beasts,
and I go to the beach cinema and watch anything, whatever,
and drink a lemonade when I get out and look at the stars
over the sea and think that the actor playing Pablo Neruda
was more handsome and taller than Neruda himself, and I write a
    postcard
sitting at a terrace, and order a gin with ice,
and then another, and then three more, and I want it all back,
the age of words and the age of innocence,
both of them back together, but I am an old-fashioned vampire,
one who has been dead as long as he has been alive;
an inexpert vampire, prodigal, with no crimes worth remembering.

Once again I find it hard to stand up, and I ask God to give me a
    second
chance, but why would he want to, if I just go back to misusing
everything like I always do, better to carry on as a fair-weather
vampire: daytime lightning in my soul, kings
from the days of the Spanish Reconquista who rot with me
in Purgatory, Third Reich officials, Cervantes and Goya,
a ninety-seven year old nun dead in a convent
left to ruin, whose funeral was attended by a black vampire
with a red rose, the start and end of all movement, order, nothing,
avarice, chaos, lust, the sunflowers' dry instant.

My love do not leave me, the night is large and I am feverish;
all my wicked deeds conspire and I never wish to lose my life.

My love do not leave me, die in my stead if you must,
although I wouldn't know how to do anything without you.

My love do not leave me, life will never end and the day
has too many hours, so much light, and I was always alone,
and there is nothing on earth to cure what I suffer,
God has left me too long alone with myself.

I don't believe it is night-time,
I don't believe in the ice in my glass of white gin,
I don't believe in the promenade where I sit,
I am nothing and I want it like that, because there has never been
    anything;
I loved art, I hated art, the moon came out and I kept on drinking
and I was happy.

The Swimmer

A black Arab comes onto the terrace facing the sea.
His skin is still wet; he has come from bathing and he sits next to me
and says in enviable Spanish, in a secret and sonorous voice:
you know, I have nothing, I own nothing, and I could have had it all,
you can tell men apart by what drives them, some want
money and power, some want fame and rewards, want to triumph,
*   succeed;*
other men want pleasure, still others want an honest job
and to start a family, others save up for a bigger car,
others want a divorce and a younger bride,
but I, believe me, all I want to do is talk to you,
want you to know that everything is a lie, that even art
and music are lies, that the air you breathe is a lie,
and I have only realised that now, coming out of the water;
I have been in the sea all morning, look at how my hands
are wrinkled, I swam very far out, and then I came back, I could have
stayed out there, but I came back and when I climbed tired from the sea,
tired and sad, I saw you on this terrace and looked at your eyes
and you made me sad because I know you are truly alone,
that you sleep alone, eat alone, drink alone.

What more did you see out there, in the middle of the sea,
after swimming all morning? I ask him.
And he replies: *I've already told you I could have stayed out there,*
dead or alive, drowned or turned to a wave of blood;
I saw that I matter as much dead as alive, alive as much as dead,
and in this moment there came to my eyes my parents' eyes
on the day I was born, and I felt free, too free.
But if you want to know what the sea said to me, OK,
this is what the sea said: 'None of you is any better
that any other, and you will all die. You all lack
the slightest capacity for grandeur, not a single one of you
is exceptional, you are all worth the same.'

The black Arab gets up from his chair and leaves. I order a gin
with ice and lemon and drink until night comes, without eating.
Drunk, terribly drunk, I order the key to my room

at reception, I am very dizzy, I go out onto the balcony
of my room facing the sea – I had to pay double
to get a seaview – and I feel a painful desire to fuck
three women at the same time: I must be dying
in the middle of the sea, but it is true, all the institutions
of the earth are an annoying lie,
just as the black Arab said, although he did not reveal the worst.
The worse, unarguably, is that it doesn't matter, because the whole
    world
believes absolutely in the lie. It could be that the only ones who don't
are he and I: he in the water, six hours swimming,
like in that film *The Swimmer*, from pool to pool,
from beach to beach; and I, drinking, from hotel to hotel,
gin upon gin, the two of us completely alone,
and who would love us, if we don't believe in anything,
if we are obsessed with what we were, believing
that it is in what we were that can be found the reason for this lack
    of faith?
Let's hope no one loves us, and we can carry on swimming,
because it is good to swim, because to swim in the sea,
in July, is something very beautiful.

Mallorca

I was in Mallorca as well, and bought a ticket for the Valldemosa
Charterhouse, and went – for free – to the tomb of Robert Graves,
who chose Spain as one might choose a set of fishknives for the
    wedding
of some distant relatives.

Chopin and his slut of a girlfriend walked through here in winter
pyjamas and didn't touch each other, and didn't dream of the
    millions
of tourists who would come here a hundred years later.
If they had done so they would have bought half the island.

The sea grows confused at dusk, and gives me heroes from olden
    days,
and from my past, and I see myself in my smock at playtime
at the Piarist school; I see myself making love to a Chinese woman,
whom a friend from back then paid for.
I see myself working as a builder to pay for my studies
which, obviously, did not help me become rich.
I see myself with teary eyes when I found out that Anabel,
my girlfriend when we were fifteen, had died on the road, crushed
by a lorry, and the whole class went to the burial
and she stayed there, in the shadows,
in her bad luck, in the theft or loss of her life.
I will never enjoy what I was going to enjoy, and the sea of existence
separates us forever. She stayed dead, and I was alive;
she was frozen and I grew like a tree.
Her eyes were like lilac, she went to the vast kingdom of snow
buried underground, snow in a tomb that will never thaw,
and I stayed here, in the streets, the shops and the bars.

I hired a Ford Ka with air conditioning and went to Porto Cristo.
I spent all afternoon in the water, and my skin burnt, and I could not
calm the heat, and I left the water and drank gin with ice
and paid a bill of eighty thousand pesetas; I was drinking
and eating rock mussels and gilt-heads and clams and lobster,
until the day came, and then,

with sand in my eyes and on my lips,
I swam out to the horizon and saw my skin burn
and it was July, the eternal cloud of summer;
I love it when you don't wear panties,
when you sit at the hotel table, brown-skinned and happy,
semi-naked from the waist upwards, when you eat
some philosophical salad and I know that under your clothes
is that which so excited Pedro Salinas
and which he could not describe
without using what we all use: metaphors.

And tomorrow you are going to New York and you say
that you will never forget me, and both things are true,
and that is what Spanish beaches have always been for.
You go back to your job as a saleswoman in the
Carolina Herrera shop in Manhattan.
New York has fifteen million faces;
you will lose your tan, you will put up the poster from the Dragon
    Caves
and hide the photograph
that you took of me on the sand,
when you said that it looked like
the Lighthouse at Alexandria.

I have no money to go to New York;
I spent it all on a week in Mallorca;
I am a gentleman of the peninsula,
and only have just enough to send you this postcard of heaven,
as some other poet once put it.

And you, every Christmas, as a token of your memory,
send me from America a complete set
(gel, cologne, aftershave) of Carolina Herrera *For Men*.
And you don't know how well it suits me or how long it lasts.

Heaven

At the end of a very long corridor you will see God, who will greet you calmly, will hug you, and will show you the slow meaning of any man's life, because all men are one man. Before your very eyes, God will show you life before history and life after history, an algebra of flesh and spirit. You will fall in love. The moment at which you fall in love will open into a hundred moments, and these will open into a thousand, and these into a hundred thousand... You will see snow, and the dream that made snow, the whim of snow, the divine and ironic moments of inspiration which make up the make-up of all that is made up and the final drop of infinity, humble infinity, simple, poor, needy. Everything will rise up before your eyes, and the questions which tormented you will be resolved like a child's game. And even when this has been fulfilled along with hundreds of other unnameable desires, you will not be happy for more than a few weeks or months, or years, the time it takes to play your way into a new game but no longer. In fact you can never be happy even after God has shown you what can't even be dreamt of. And you will not suffer if God does not show you the great hidden wonders of history, of mankind and of life, if you want to put it like that. However wonderful that which is shown you, your happiness is transitory. Sleep in your bed, shut up, sleep, drink and shut up, like an animal. Like an animal, who will not know the resurrection of the flesh, or evil, or love, or law, or grace: things which are alien and yet innocent.

Memory is black as well, like those African hookers who sleep with you for a thousand bucks, and obey you with a kind of bitter docility, and all of this comes from the hand of God. Stand by the window so that my neighbour can see you, you said to her, stand there naked and show him your pussy so they can see the slut you are and so his wife can call the police and put in a complaint for offences against public decency. Dance a little behind the curtains. It is impossibly hot. *Humble infinity, poor, needy, love's beggar, the beggar of any love, of the cheapest kind of love.*

I go out into the street, I stand at a high café table and order a martini and some olives. My body is sweating: it is the glory of summer, the feast of our needs, the joy of all those who will live. Happiness, glory, resurrection, beauty, innocence, happiness, joy, exaltation, pleasure, majesty, splendour, heaven. Never forget that heaven exists. Go out and live, thinking of heaven, look for it; it is permitted for a man to spend his life in trying to be happy. Nothing else matters. Go forth and be happy. Be very happy.

Beech Grove

(Valle del Aspe, August 1998)

God granted the middle classes fine weather and the summer
so that they could enjoy the beach, water and light,
as hope for and prophecy of an incomparable future,
far superior to the splendour and government of tyrants.
Life, and Spain, have always been filled with tyrants.

And so the workers and the office drones came to the seaside,
or down to the river or the lake, with hats and cheap hammocks,
with food brought from home, with their drinks in the coolbox,
with new sandals, with their flower-patterned bathing caps,
with newspapers, with cigars, with moustaches peeping over their
    lips.

I don't want to carry on writing poetry. I don't believe in it.
It is a coward's vocation, something for helpless legislators.
Poetry has stopped serving man to serve instead the history
of poetry, which is an old temptation of mankind,
a ridiculous bore, an empty glass somewhere at midnight.
I spend my life buying flick-knives.

I look at myself in the mirror at the Hotel Bernadette;
I am wearing white, and a silk tie,
like a communicant with the rosary and the cross
in his hands, earthly, clear, exalted and it isn't even
eleven a.m. and I have already drunk
with inappropriate liberality, my lavish hand on the bottle.

I look at myself in the dirty mirror at the Sahara Inn,
Marrakesh, and the red carpet on the floor is nearly blood,
the towels don't take the sweat from my body,
and the water burns and is poisoned.

The beech grove is offended and reminds me of the past.
I look for raspberries and cranberries in the beech grove.
I wanted to be here, down at ground level, like the beeches,

like oak trees and ash trees and silver firs.
Trees are like the dead.

My past is a river, a watermill, a flick-knife, a fishing rod.

The Unknown Man

On an August night, in Cadaqués, I fell to drinking
with an unknown man. It got to be six in the morning,
we went down to the beach with a bottle of gin,
and there was already that horrible unsleeping heat,
the old age of desire.

The unknown man looked at the stars and spoke without meaning;
there was a boat up on the sand and he threw little stones at it
while he drank and smoked.
The unknown man had come with me from bar to bar,
and had taken on a lot of gin with me,
both of us prisoners of the sea and these boats of physical
    exhaustion,
speaking of women and football, telling jokes and moving our feet
rhythmically, one hand holding
a Bic biro, and the other the glass of gin.

The unknown man said *it is already growing light, it'll cool down soon;*
I used to have a good job and earned quite a lot of money
and my mother was proud of me.
I was good at my work and dedicated my whole life to it.
One day my mother fell ill and the doctors told me
she was going to die; but that it would be a long, slow death, unpredictable.
I gave up as many of my obligations as possible to look after her,
my bosses asked me about my mother almost every day,
but I realised I couldn't be out of the office
much longer and hired a nurse.
One night my mother got much worse, but the next morning
she told me that she was better and I went to work,
and while I was in my office working, my mother died.
I didn't see her die and I was not with her when she died.
I got back home and she was dead.

Six months later they sacked me
because my department was no longer viable
and I was even less viable
because I had grown melancholy,

unbearable, lazy, alcoholic, violent.
I gave my flesh and my mother's flesh for this job
and then they sent me into limbo.

I'm not going to feel sorry for you, I said.
If you don't have a place to sleep, sleep on the beach.
I've already paid fifteen rounds of gin, and six packs of Marlboros,
and I do have somewhere to sleep, a three star hotel,
which isn't bad: the showers are strong enough
and the sheets and towels are much cleaner than your soul.
But, you know, if it would help, I'll say I'm sorry about your mother,
and if I had a copy of Jorge Manrique's poetry here with me
I'd give it to you straight away, because Manrique was this guy
who lost his father like you lost your mother,
but he didn't have a bad job like you,
and definitely drank a lot less than you do.
And Manrique, poet and warrior, would have known to slash the
        throats
of all your bosses, the ones who stopped you from taking
your mother's hand when she left this world.
That's what's killing you now, that you weren't brave enough
to kill the people who misled you and brought you into
a false life, a life without honour.

The unknown man stands up
and throws an empty bottle of gin into the sea,
then he takes off his shirt, and naked enters
the water with decisive strides, *goodbye*, he says,
I'm walking to the end of the earth,
and then a wave hits him and knocks him over.

He is so drunk that as he falls
he breaks open his head on a rock on the seabed.
His body inert, the waves soaking his clothes on the sand,
his head and his hair filled with blood,
the gin mixed with blood and the blood mixed with water,
I call the police and a doctor says that the unknown man
has snuffed it, that he was so drunk
the blow to his head choked him,
and I look at him and yes, he looks like he can't breathe.

They take me to the police station and I get back to my hotel at
    seven p.m.,
tired, dirty, having signed a hundred statements, with a cheque
for forty dollars made out to a young man
who has been lawyer for me,
tired of cafes and sub-commissaries,
I throw myself down on the hotel bed and fall asleep,
thinking about the unknown man's mother, about meetings
between the dead, the dead mother, the dead son, everyone dead,
and all the time my fellow hotel-dwellers taking the sun on the
    terrace
and the hotel orchestra – it is a tourist hotel – starts
to set up by the swimming pool, and I am lost
in this world like a beast with no heart, like an infantry captain
in the Great War with his chest unseamed by bullets,
with a huge moustache, with dark eyebrows, wide-shouldered,
a captain who seems dead, but who suddenly
leaps from the trench and starts to shoot at everyone,
and it is impossible that a man with so many bullets in him
could still even hold a pistol.

Light

The afternoon light came in, showing off against the little bottles
in the hotel minibar, a mountain light –
we are in the most expensive hotel in the Alps – which brought
  with it the cold
at the end of August. From the terrace *put on a jumper if you're*
  going out
onto the balcony you could see those pine trees, huge, religious,
  fragments
of an innocent god's flesh, *why don't you want to see anyone,*
you antisocial bastard, spending all your time shut up here, drinking
and looking at the pine trees? you asked me, and I replied firmly
because I'm fucking dead, I'm just a corpse travelling
the world, a bastard on his eternal holiday, a ravisher
of luxury hotel minibars, a consumer of miniatures,
and all I care about is this light, this light that fills the room
because this light is the most mysterious thing I have ever seen,
it's like you could hold in it the life I have lived
and the life I have not lived, all mixed together, a transparent ghost.

Your skirt, your black panties on the chair, you're sitting on the floor
drinking a gin and tonic, *if I didn't like you so much,* you said, *come*
  here,
let's go back to bed, and I started to eat your arms,
your hands, your well-trimmed nails, and the light kept coming
and shone on the labels of the little bottles
from the minibar. *You're a dirty man, you son of a bitch, not like that,*
dirty man, you kept on saying, but the light never went away.

And she, who had spoken of her life and her dreams,
with her underwear scattered over the room,
scattered decently, her still complaining
about how, instead of going out, we stayed fucking
all night long, and then, saturated, saying this,
dirty man, son of a bitch, I told you not to do that
to me again, calling me all night long, saying the same thing.

I slept for a while, then got up from the bed, naked,
went to the minibar, took the last miniature and drank it at a gulp,
went to the bathroom and ran the tap till it came out cold
then drank, and soaked my mouth and my tongue for a long time,
you were still asleep, I still had your juices all over my body,
your saliva and the liquid of your sex and your mouth, Scottishing
    me,
and the light had already gone, bringing instead a patient darkness.

HEAT

(2008)

I ain't gone away yet
The Who (2004)

Rain

Madrid, 22 May 2004

We saw the '53 Rolls with its white wheels
(fifty years; one thousand kilometres)
on the TV screens in the bars in Actur, Zaragoza.
I was holding a glass of cold white wine,
and Spain was already hot;
the Mediterranean hotels were being spring-cleaned,
rooms all opened, painstaking chambermaids all waiting
for the arrival of six hundred thousand Englishmen,
a million Germans, four hundred thousand French,
a hundred thousand Swiss and a hundred thousand Belgians.
We had white wine in our hands and our necks
craned towards the TV set.

Elizabeth II of England did not come; Elizabeth II
would only accept an invitation to the King of France's wedding
and, as France has no King, Elizabeth II
stays now and forever in her palace, leaning back against the world.
It is Elizabeth II's subjects who love the Spanish sun and cheap beer,
who hang out the British flag
in their bars by the seaside.

Crepuscular royal houses, plucked
from the rustiest corners of history
appeared on Spanish televisions on 22 May 2004:
Nordic countries, distant and wealthy, cold and cut off
from this ever-embracing heart.
Rouco Varela leading the mass.
The President of the French Republic did not come.
The archbishops, two-tone, happy.
The Lord's name spoken out loud many times.
This obstinate obsession with naming God, naming Him
as one might give a name to power, or money,
or the Resurrection, the guillotine, prison, slavery.
The Emperor of the World stayed in America,
uninterested in the minor rituals of his provinces.

The huge blue umbrellas.
                    To get up at six o'clock in the morning
so they can put on makeup, depilate you, give you a manicure:
what a joy.
The vast breakfasts, the silver cutlery,
the finest wines and the extraordinary colognes.
The gigantic shower-rooms, the suites, the Swiss chocolates,
the golden slippers, the platinum underwear,
the orange juice made from vile oranges.
Luxury and service, people always opening doors for you.
Permanent smiles.
The professionals with their permanent smiles,
smiles that represent the most inhospitable job in history.
Smile? What for?

And Umbral, and Gala, and Bosé, and A., and J., and Ayala, and
    M.M.
all walking into the Catedral de la Almudena,
rewarded, chosen,
seated on the right, the preeminent figures of Spanish *savoir-faire*,
of Spain's ascent, of its great growth.
The great ascent, the great ascension.
And the hundred and ninety people burnt alive had their homage
    paid them:
this absurd and mutilated populace, this Goyaesque populace
both elemental and monarchist;
the Rolls passed in front of them.
And the former President of the Republic drank a '94 Rioja Reserva;
all of the former Presidents of Spain, each with his jacket,
and his wife in the background,
protective, ravenous, eternally
interchangeable, but happy to have made it this far,
so far, all the way here where the air is gold and your hand can
    grasp the world,
here, where the whole of Spain wanted them to be
and democratic legitimacy is an absolute blazon.

Iridescent sun-hats, yokes on people's heads,
yokes under a darkening sky.

And José María Aznar and Jordi Pujol
and Felipe González, together again.
And the three of them felt happy to see a job well done,
Franco's succession, the European hand, paternal,
laid on our heads,
Franco's succession, the Francoist *mantillas*
put away in wardrobes,
screeching with envy and breathing the whitest naphtha.
And Juan Carlos I stuck carrying the weight of Spain,
because who would carry Spain if he did not,
who would carry Spain's history, the papal seal on his little finger.
And Zapatero with his wife Sonsoles, voluptuous, smiling,
the kind of woman who would have suited Baudelaire or Julio
     Romero.
Sonsoles looked like a Delacroix:
a close-fleshed Liberty guiding the people,
show-off sun-hats, the political ritual,
the boredom of history,
sagging tits.

And socialists and liberals and ultramontanists all together,
the left and the right muddled together,
salaries all expanded to satiety,
everyone looking for the same thing, Sonsoles looked like a
     Delacroix,
the new Queen of Spain,
Queen of office provision, of glories,
of long trips across the world in official aircraft,
of lay fortunes.
Atheists transformed in the blaze from the sun-hats,
believers with atheist wallets.
Power at all times always equal to itself.
Human history throughout time similar to how it was a while back.
The same time at all times.
The essence of Spain repeating itself, the essence of the wide world.

And all of us drinking in Actur, next to the cranes and the
     supermarket,
happy they allow us to drink this wine,

this cold wine, from a half-clean glass, happy
to have the money for this wine and then two more.

And the abused pallor of Queen Rania of Jordan.
And the rain.

HU-4091-L

Farewell, my brother; the funeral crane carries you
to scrapyard hell.
Majestic, you move towards your destruction
on a red crane,
as though you were Louis XVI on his way to the guillotine,
with me walking behind you.
You are like a king.
I am the only one who has come to see you buried.

I have loved you.
I said a Pater Noster and an Ave Maria for you.
I prayed for you and I was moved.
You were the best.
And yes, the life we lived together, the cities we criss-crossed,
the B roads we drove and the villages
and oceans we saw,
and the underground carparks and the freezing tunnels
through the mountainside, sharpened
stalactites at the entry
that threatened our miraculous innocence,
and the beggars in the avenues,
                              asking for money when the lights were red,
and how, in the darkness of the motorways, we loved each other,
blent to a single being: your flesh joining with my radiator badge.

You saved me from acid rain and from snow without angels.
Your air-conditioning, which is still intact
after twelve years, saved me
from being burnt alive in Spanish summers.
Ay, the cold air blown round my feet.
And you were white,
for sanctity and industrial love and speed are all white.
And how I liked to move up through the gears,
and how you went up into fifth, and the pace you had on you,
narcissist, you were such a narcissist.

And now it is all over.

We were together for two hundred and sixty-eight thousand
    kilometres.
We were happy.
We were great and emblematic.
I give you a kiss in front of the scrap metal merchant
and a black man
who carries a leaking radiator in one hand.
I have loved you more than my lovers,
more than my dog;
almost as much, but not quite, eh, as I love money.

Alright, don't get cross:
you were money yourself once,
and you still are,
and I am money myself as well.

Forgive me if I humble you by dropping
onto your fine upholstery,
onto your wheels, all the couplings
and valves that have so gloriously burnt out:
the destitution of Spain:
zero percent finance, a grant of 400 euros
for the middle classes,
who all love a handout
(are you upset that I talk about money, or just about so little money?).

You, who were my freedom, who brought me close to paradise;
you, who spoke to me at night, and said to me
brother, how well you drive; brother,
you truly are the best of men.

The Tree of Life

(Christmas 2006)

This time of year I mix the living with the dead. I mix expensive aftershave with even more expensive cologne, this time of year. I think about the thirty million euros I've earned this year to date and I laugh; I feel happy when I think about Spanish widows with their pensions of 400 euros a month. I think that they must be like supermarket own-brand mince pies, and a huge laugh, the white gas of happiness, burns through my lungs. I spend Christmas Eve in a Manhattan apartment: three hundred and eighty-nine square metres not counting the balconies, those mysterious balconies under an indifferent moon. I give a party for elegant Jews and we talk about Faulkner and Dante. Then I throw one of these Jews through a window, from the ninetieth floor. I spend New Year's Eve in the Castellana Suite of the Old Hilton in Havana, and chat with Fidel about Camilo Cienfuegos and Ernesto (those holy dead who will never be touched by disappointment); revolutionary flags on the tables, covered with tropical fruit; panoramic sea-views and elaborate nostalgia for Che, who played chess here, in this suite on the twenty-second floor, his smile always Byronic. I call Benedict XVI from Havana and we chat for a while, and I ask him about the end of the world: he laughs; he knows my little jokes. 'It's on its way,' Benny says, and then adds, 'but don't you worry, your future's already secure.' Long secret passages in the Vatican, with God at one end of them, in the sad dark of the unbreakable alcoves. I spend Epiphany in Paris, in the Chopin Suite in the Ritz. There's still something of him there, some fossilised bacteria, remnant of his equally fossilised tuberculosis. I'm never in Spain over the festive period; it's too depressing. Although I do speak to the Spanish King on New Year's Day. 'You should declare yourself emperor as soon as possible, like our dear friend Hirohito: these people really don't deserve anything else.' I'm sad I can't speak with Stalin anymore; I miss him so much. I can't cope with how boring the world is. These are terrible times. There is nothing left of the world any more. There are only motorways, policemen and traffic lights. Millions of traffic lights, all stuck on red. Traffic lights manufactured in industrial estates outside Munich, Madrid, Moscow, Manchester, Milan.

These traffic lights are all there is; we have spent millions of years waiting for them to change. There are domestic appliances, and the unemployed, and Chinese people and scrap iron and empty tyres, the air forced out of them, tyres that have come down from the still-emptier clouds, clouds with no liquid in them, clouds filled with burning trash risen up from the earth. No revolution in the offing. No social class that attempts to rise from the filth. This vast plain of filth. Tyrants are not put to the firing squad. There aren't even any tyrants. The adolescent daughters of neurotic queens are not raped. There are secretaries of residents' associations. Universal boredom. People turn forty, and then they turn fifty. And then they die and it is as though they had never lived. Rich and poor, the living and the dead. Evil really gets on my tits.

Brotherhood

I like the bright-lit streets of the city on Saturday night, when winter arrives and people decide to live.

I'm seduced by the smell of mozzarella and oregano from the pizzerias.

I am crazy about 500 euro notes. All kinds of life are good. I love the King of Spain's Field Marshal, his uniform when he goes out on manoeuvres.

I love the swimmers who swim naked, out in the Pacific, under a compassionate sun, waiting for the sky to fall on their frozen shoulders.

I love the desire to swim.

I used to love Communist women swimmers because they won all the gold medals at the Olympic Games and didn't speak English and lived in grey little flats and their cars were made out of wood. I adored their swimming costumes, their bathing caps, the way they greeted the Communist fatherland from the victor's podium. I was mad about the former Soviet Union and the German Democratic Republic. I adored General Jaruzelski, his big old-fashioned spectacles.

I adored the Communists, their red get-up, the red star on their marble foreheads, their fortified nature. I am a vulture in love. No problems with me, I'm charm itself, d'you get me?, no problems with someone like me.

I am the best of men.

If your wife leaves you, I'll drink with you all night and get you calm again, because I'm a good guy and I love you. I love you all, men and women. I love being here, like a sturdy oak. Here with you. It's enough for me to be here with you, it was happiness itself. I love official cars when they turn up on television. I'm crazy about the President's eternally new shoes. I love the haircuts and perfume and necklaces and almost Babylonian handbags that female ministers carry. While we're at it, I adore Babylon.

I kiss this good world. For the world is good. Really, the world is perfect. I don't do irony, just love. I'm telling you, just love for everything. I am adoration itself. Day and night, I adore life. Legendary adoration.

I adore the material of our holy life.

I adore cities, houses, furniture, children, avenues.

I don't want to die, I don't want to leave, this is all done in honour of me.

I'd let them cut my throat for you, because you are alive and I want you to stay alive. Because I adore you.

I fall in love with cities. I talk to the living and the dead. I'm not looking out for knowledge, no. I don't know peace, I don't want to know anything. It is a great thing to say *no* to knowledge. That is the love I am looking for. Not the usual kind, that's true. How lucky. Lucky. Lucky. How great.

I fall in love with the lifts in luxury hotels, impossibly clean, smelling of abundant, serene, Category A industrial perfume at eight-thirty a.m. and I think about the tormented hands of the cleaners, earning a pittance; I think of their rings and bracelets.

I fall in love with waitresses, tortured, abused.

I love the sun, streets with the sun shining on them.

How wonderful that the sun exists; I conceive you, sun.

How wonderful that stars exist; I conceive them; I forgive them for their distance, I forgive them, I forgive them their nonappearance in this hand, in this flesh.

I adore waitresses and their role in human history. I love escalators: I love standing on them, borne upwards, meditating, like a quadriplegic sultan. I adore quadriplegics. I adore people with cerebral palsy. I adore the blind. I love all invalids, the mentally deficient, the people whom this world, or any other world, has destroyed. I love the new ATMs, with their green keypads, grandiose, spreading light, taking out money, lots of money, all the money.

I have no peace, I know no peace.

I adore Frankenstein – that student genius – *mon semblable, mon frère*. I love old people. I love old people's homes, built in the new suburbs round Madrid, Seville, Barcelona, Bilbao, Malaga, Valencia and Zaragoza.

I love cities, because I love anything that is larger than my body.

I have no peace, of course not, that's fine. I know no peace, I don't know what peace is, I haven't had the pleasure. I'm lucky not ever to have known it. I'm lucky not to know anything: the blindness of the living, of course.

I loved Istanbul, I was a neurotic there as well, like I was in New

York, and I ate lots of spicy meat and used up all the towels in the hotel, rubbing them against my skin until I shredded them, until skin and cotton were mixed together.

I loved having my breakfast completely naked – the air in mourning – on a terrace looking out over the Bosporus, and I would really have loved to convert to Islam because I was already bored of Catholicism and I let my beard grow and wore rings and bracelets I had bought in the Grand Bazaar.

If I had been born in Istanbul, I would have been poor there as well, I would have had to drag myself after groups of tourists, selling knives made of wood and counterfeit perfume, selling counterfeit bracelets and watches and shirts and belts and underwear. I adore counterfeit goods. The world is a permanent counterfeit.

Only poverty is large as the sun, large as snow and blood.

I have adored the food of the poor, I adored the barbecued fish that they sold for a euro each on the banks of the Golden Horn and I didn't care about swallowing the bones which scratched my tongue that was always thirsty for everything.

And I swam, in love with no one, in the Sea of Marmara and asked once again to drown, but Istanbul didn't want my death: *we are glorious and we are ubiquitous, don't be afraid of being alone, you are nothing but lechery because everything was lechery, from the very first atom of oxygen before life came into being.* And I had another barbecued fish, for a euro. It was so cheap, and these common fish were a delicacy, eaten next to the fire, by the water.

For forty-four years I have seen God in cities filled with clouds, with baked clay, with sun, with hatred, with love, with iron faces. I have long conversations with cities. I spoke with Istanbul, the both of us sitting on the steps of Hagia Sofia, the both of us damp and humble, looking at the shields on the columns.

I have no peace, I know no peace.

And I loved Seville, and I swam in the Guadalquivir, swimming by the industrial oil shore, amid the toxic waste. I love trash, because poetry is now to be found in the trash. I loved the air over Chernobyl just as I will love the white guts of the last Canadian whale.

I love the meat that they throw away in high-end restaurants: huge black plastic bins with vast blue bags inside them, piled full of steaks and lobsters that rich people have left on their vast and shining plates. I am moved by the food that is abandoned in Paris every day: ten thousand kilos of innocent beef, imported from Argentina, needlessly dead.

Everything that comes from man – war, sickness, science, love, history, cosmetics, swimming costumes – I love it all.

All I can do is love. I don't know how to judge. I am nothing but infatuation. A lover, a lover who has loved men and women who have had no effect on the flow of history, who have no power or wealth or prestige or cunning or intelligence.

Let me kiss your iron face.

I have no peace, I know no peace.

I adore all those who didn't deserve to be adored while they were alive and who don't deserve to be adored now, being dead, because no one deserves anything.

I have no peace, I know no peace.

I love the doves from the Plaza del Pilar in Zaragoza, stinking, right at the top of the tallest towers, not wanting to come down, presiding over the stupid planetary light that burns for the living and the dead. Not wanting to come down.

I love the green and gold Ray-Bans that I use to protect my eyes from the radiation of life. I love seeing the venomous flow of all things and the strange kiss of the moon.

I feel that I am everything's brother. Brother of those who died in hatred. Brother of the ones who were murdered. Brother of those who died without having lived. Brother of Africa and Asia.

Brother of the Blacks, the Chinese and the Indians.

You're lucky to have me as a brother because I am the best. Brother of oppressed peoples, keen to oppress them even more until they are turned into hurricanes and tempests and typhoons and catastrophes.

My heart is a shop window filled with trinkets from the East and the West.

My heart is a Russian steppe, with automatic weapons.

My heart is a revolution, full of hangings, firing squads, millions of blows rained down on the innocent.

I kiss all the innocent.

I love all the innocent.

I would die for them without thinking about it for a fraction of a second.

I will never pass judgement on life.

I will love and I will not be responsible.

I kiss the ones who have nothing.
I kiss the ones who have lost it all.
I kiss those whom no one will kiss.

I kiss the light.

Let me kiss your marble lips.
I kiss all the innocent.

Mazda 6

Manuel Vilas went out of his house one morning.
He was expected at a high school somewhere in Zaragoza.
He was going to speak
to the students, who had all read his poems.
A high school on the outskirts of town, as it always was.

He drove down the Avenida de Madrid, where blazed
shops crammed with marked-down goods: shoes, bags, clothes,
vast red signs that mentioned 'impossible' prices –
this was in March, the beginning of the month, and it was already
    hot.
It was early, so he had a coffee in a bar filled with people
having breakfast: croissants, buns, little sandwiches, toast, jam,
    butter.
And Manuel Vilas did not pay for his coffee
because of divine indolence,
because he did not make the effort
to call for the waitress,
the effort to take out his wallet
and look for a single coin.
And it didn't matter that he left without paying
and this put him in an excellent mood
which lasted for thirty seconds, the thirty seconds
of glorious flight, the glory of thieves lost
in distant suburbs, in slow-beating hearts.
He went into the classroom and said hello to the kids who had all
    read his poems.
They were seventeen years old,
boys and girls, attractive, brand new, filled with a great sweetness.
The kids looked at him with violent curiosity, and Manuel Vilas
remembered that he had brushed up well that morning.
He spoke, and didn't know rightly what to say.
As he spoke, he looked out through a large window
which showed blocks of flats from the sixties,
with flowers and bicycle wheels on little balconies,
houses for immigrants now, and he realised once more
how much Spain had visibly changed,

this great party that was Spain, the great party made of heat and
    summer,
a party where few were invited,
as always.

A girl asked him why there was so much sex in his poems.

A boy asked him who the protagonist of his poems was.

Another girl asked him why he wrote about New York in his poems.

Another boy asked him why he wrote about money in his poems.

Manuel Vilas looked at these boys and girls with a fascination worthy
of the first microsecond after the creation of the earth,
after the creation of the volcanoes,
the creation of the sky and the wind.
These are my children, he thought, the world is theirs, and so is
    blood, the oceans, the moon, all the sand on all the beaches, the
    boats, the secret trees, the dance-halls and the dark rooms, all
    the beds and all the wicked flowers.

He saw the wind blowing through the heads of the students who
    asked so many
questions.

Manuel Vilas was now thinking about his car,
a Mazda 6, red, new, metallic,
one hundred and fifty horsepower entirely at his disposal.
He thought that he had left it parked under a tree,
and thought, yes, about how good it must be for his Mazda 6
to be under a tree,
and as they were talking about literature
he remembered Virgil and imagined Virgil
under a Roman olive tree two thousand years before,
happy to be alive.

And now the students had grown tired of asking questions,
and they were talking

about how time passes and cities as well,
Manuel Vilas asked them a question:
*Tell me how the world will be
in a hundred years' time, in 2107.
And tell me how it must have been in 1907.*

He told his students that they had to be happy to be alive.
He repeated the verb 'to be', yes.
That it was wonderful to be alive,
that there was nothing else so wonderful.

Manuel Vilas got into his Mazda 6 and stroked the manes
of the hundred and fifty horses entirely at his disposal,
ready to throw themselves against the gates of heaven if he so desired.

He remembered the students, his foot pressing the accelerator.
He saw the wind blowing through the heads of the students
who had asked him so many questions.

Cocaine

Light of the city we drink you at night.

We make love so close to the kitchen –
this flat is so small –
that the smell of the drains comes through like an odour of sanctity,
dirty and sticky,
crooked, synthetic,
too hot...
all over your body with its tattoos and fishscales.

Light of the city you are white as the sun.

I know people, fifty-five years old or thereabouts,
in important jobs under the city lights:
people who speak perfect Spanish;
contented people with a position in society,
who never make love like you and I make love
(if this is love and not a lie),
with these cries forced from us
(if they are cries rather than stories):
forced from our skin, our language, from the acid
of these enigmatic tiles on the floor;
people who barely love like this, as we do –
with anger and no future, rage and no compassion –
and I do not understand how life could be other
than the white hair
on your hypocritical and regally unconcealed flesh
as though the national anthems of France and Germany,
Russia and Spain, of Sweden, of Finland,
were blaring out not in any Olympic Games
but rather in the heart of these industrial suburbs.

Light of the city we drink you at night.

Sometimes we do not sleep in the small hours and think of Mars
and think of the ashes rising from the crematoria
(carbonised bodies, people born to decorate the sky

and seeking their grave in the contaminated air,
the air filled with human ashes rising from the ground:
tongues and arses, femurs and sacra, livers and semen);
spend seven solid hours looking at the gilded rosette in the ceiling
of a bedroom doused in the noises
of ancient, faraway cars,
or of our neighbours opening and closing their doors;
and we look out of the window,
sensing through the frame
the strength of the cranes that build life and history.

Light of the city I drink you defenceless.

When I am seventy,
cut me wide open,
and throw my heart to the dogs.
And you, eat with them,
fight with them to let you sink your teeth in,
bite it like you know how,
bitch,
bite my heart.

I love you.

I love you so much.

I love you
like dinosaurs love the light that falls from stars,
love to drink it at night;
like lions in Africa gorge themselves on zebras with their dirt-filled
    kidneys;
like white men eat blacks with their hearts filled with white men's
    dreams.

Light of the city, you are my lover, my mirror, my joy.

I spend my nights screaming.
Against the darkness, against the moon,
screaming.

Take your clothes off, bitch:
screams in the small hours of the night,
in the stairwells of terrible apartment blocks:
praise, far too much praise.

Everything is white.

Take your clothes off, you dog. Are you shivering? Do I scare you?

Light of the city we drink you at night.

Light of the city that illuminates
the dogs,
the blacks,
the children,
the saints,
the resurrected,
the old,
the poor,
the murderers,
the women,
the unilluminable women.

Light of the city we drink you at night.

Light of the city over your *aschenes Haar Shulamith*.

Tonight I want so much.
I'll kill you. I'll give it you. I'll give you this.
We'll get married. I'll give it you, I swear.

I love you.

AIDS

I.

It's like the whole world is on fire, but only I am burning.
Do you hear me? I am burning, in madness, which belongs
to the kingdom of life, and is life itself, and only happens if you are
    alive.
I am a most illegal being (playing with words to the very end),
and life made me like that. The desires of the flesh,
the small desire I had to think, I wouldn't know how to defend
    myself,
take my hand,
it is hard.
Everything was lust. A great neurosis.
Heat is lust.

I would have liked
to kiss all human beings.

I couldn't kiss them all
and I suffered.

I would have liked to kiss
an ocean, a desert and a continent.

Heat is the enemy of civilisation,
Nietzsche said, and he was thinking about Spain.

The planet is heating up, and will burn, but I am already burning,
soon it will be fifty degrees in the shade.
I have adored so many things,
and have been so selfish,
as irresponsible as a dead-end river
that will never flow to the sea,
oh, and as untrustworthy as those summer days
when you and I, my sister,
drove off the road in the red Peugeot
and ended up in the middle of a river,

and opened the doors and took the sun,
and by the water we picked ripe August blackberries,
from the brambles,
naked and dirty,
with river-mud in our mouths,
eating dragonflies out of love, out of love for insects,
for all insects,
you and I, my sister, symbolic and physical,
and now tell me why you first looked at me, yes, my sister,
tell me what you're doing
with someone like me,
with an unreadable dog such as I,
in the middle of a river,
in this gross, dry August,
with blackberries smeared
across your unpassable lips.

Oh, my sister, who are no longer my lover but rather my familiar;
you who are a mage and a medium and a witch,
you who know who I am and who know that I am nothing,
oh my sister,
unfair as I am,
liquid and resonant as I, lost
among men, lost in the cities, lost in work,
working ten hours a day to earn less than the thousand euros
that this long-form drama demands – I will not name
all your jobs here because I love you:
waitress in Charley's Girl, New Jersey,
ticket-seller in FearStore in Barcelona,
porter in the Hotel Richard III in Notting Hill, London,
survey agent, asking people about their eating habits in Móstoles,
    Madrid,
mattress saleswoman at Miracle Beds, Mexico D.F.,
burger-flipper at McDonald's, Prague, right next to Kafka,
you lasted thirty days at that one,
as you refused to learn Czech –
sitting in an ever-so-rented room,
sitting on the bed.

I heard you, my sister, leaving your days on the walls
of my ancient heart.
You look like Dostoevsky's granddaughter,
wise, and corrupted from wishing to be more wise.
Beings that are suspended forever in a pillar of warm air.
Broken beings,
beings born full of bullet holes,
of knife wounds,
of assaults against nature,
the lust of trees,
beings with accounts that have been cancelled
in wretched branches of Third World banks,
beings with passports issued
by the failed and corrupt civil servants
of stinking sultanates where the weather is foul,
where there are daily storms,
where there are daily executions,
where hands are always severed,
these incandescent beings filled with evil.

You make me despair, you, who look like
Anna Karenina's great-granddaughter,
surrounded by bony candles
steaming on your belly.
I saw your dyed hair, the hands of other men
touching your hair.
I was your husband. I was your father. I was your son.
I was your father-in-law. Your king.
Your bff, your sister, your daughter,
all your sins,
your crimes and your secrets,
your decadence,
your flesh and its clottedness,
your sad selfish empire,
your black smell.
I was your inscrutable fragility.
I was your salvation

on the day of justice,
after the resurrection of the flesh,
all mythologies fallen at your feet.

I have been mad for years,
for years it is only God who has known where I'm going,
and why my heart has become this hall of passions,
of fleshly passion in which the flesh stopped being flesh
but did not become
spirit, wing, candle, a little love,
this hall of faithless knowledge.

This real death.

They will not let us die like boys and girls swimming in the river.
We will die like old dogs in the midst of our youth.

And no one will love us,
get ready because now I'm talking to myself.

Everything is still left to do, nothing is done.
I will drag myself round the hospitals and die of fear,
I, who am still a little boy.

Like boys and girls swimming in the river,
their bicycles leaning against a tree.

I should like to be a tree.

A perfect fate.

Fate is the kiss I give you.

It was fate that I bathed in the sea, and that will survive.

The clouds.

1985

On 24 December 1985 Manuel Vilas was on duty in the Regimental Infantry Barracks in Barbastro, which was where he was doing his national service. The night watch was known as the 'reinforcements'. Vilas was in charge, and so his duty when it came to the reinforcements was to get each soldier to his sentry box and then go back to the main building.

Miguel Fernández Díaz, one of the reinforcements, whom Vilas had left at 2200 hours in sentry box number 4 (the furthest one from the main building) chose this moment to put his gun in his mouth and pull the trigger. Vilas doesn't often think about this, because it happened many years ago.

Vilas doesn't usually think about anything, and doesn't really know why he forgets things either (he thinks that it's probably because things dissolve in the memory). Vilas remembers that he stood looking at the spatters on the roof of the sentry box, all lit up by the light of a lantern. He remembers the expert commentaries from the captain about the trajectory of the bullet, and the conjectures about the hole that opened up in Fernández Díaz's head. It was a bullet from a Spanish-made Cetme rifle that transformed the youthful order of Fernández Díaz's brain into a bloody and finalised chaos.

Vilas thinks about what Miguel Fernández Díaz has missed over the last 22 years. Vilas thinks that maybe he lived through those 22 years in the 22 milliseconds it took for the bullet to untie the warm knot of his flesh. Vilas imagines himself as a radiant tourist of the past. The next day, which is to say, Christmas Day, Miguel Fernández's father came to the barracks. They hadn't been able to find his mother. There were no mobile phones in those days. No one knew where she was. The father came because someone paid for his bus ticket. Twelve hours in a bus. He was wearing a scarf.

There were no mobiles in those days, nowhere to ring.

Of course, I was the last human being to see Miguel Fernández Díaz alive. In some celestial order, perhaps it makes sense, the 'so long' he gave me back then, along with a sweet smile that was at odds with the dark night.

It was an honour, of course, that smile.

A great honour.

Because, of course, both Miguel Fernández Díaz and Manuel

Vilas Vidal were men of honour.

And honour is life.

You know something? I have the strangest sensation that it was I who fell that night, among the thousand bullets of my enemies, the bright spotlights playing in the sky over the Normandy beaches, among the absolute shrapnel, the howitzers of that ghostly artillery on this hot youthful night, and I know that there was nothing you could do for me, in spite of your risking your life for me, and the enemy sang their victory song.

Bah, you're crazy, tourism and memory, tourist in your own memory. But that kid, that kid had no luck, and he was a good kid, and I had no luck and it doesn't matter. Okay, that's it, it doesn't matter. It must be that that's killing me.

Because, yes, something is killing me.

Blood Alcohol

One night when I came back from an almighty booze-up during which I had reconciled myself to life I was given a breathalyser test by some policemen in blue uniforms and hats with worn fluorescent patches. They were guys who worked for the local council, guys with wives at home fattening themselves up for death, which rules the world; while their wives are dying they patrol the city with their roadblocks and apparatus for measuring the blood alcohol of their fellow men: a task which justifies a life of high service. They speak about football with their fellow-officers, and that is all they do. Bah, leave them alone, don't get involved, they're probably fine people. But what a bunch of … No, I don't want to be serious, I don't want to be sad; what I want is to be happy. *You know: I would have liked – trying not to get bored – to have been in Paris in 1789, in Moscow in 1917, in Madrid in 1936, burning everything down. I'm not alone. It's just that I hate it when the telephone is answered by a machine, when the traffic lights show amber, or red, or green, I hate information systems and company hierarchies and I hate legal declarations and bank transfers and civil servants putting in for transfers; I hate regional ministries for industry, the pharmaceutical industry, television cables with no television at the end of them, I even hate Christmas bonuses and a leg of ham from the boss. I hate black holes and white holes. I hate Being. I hate Nothingness. I hate hatred. And, even so, I am in love. Completely in love. And I'm lucky: I'm alive. I like to remember the man I was, I like to remember that I was the best, powerful and savage, I remember the boy I was and I see him next to me, sitting at the breathalyser station. I envy monkeys, up in their trees, taking the sun, entirely naked, with their bellies stuffed full of bananas and warm fruit and snake meat, if indeed monkeys do eat snakes, with their thoughts full of splendour, with the moon shining down on their genitals, calm up there in the sky. Satiated on the night, useless, thirsty.*

When they let me go (the breathalyser was positive, of course) it was already day. I had drunk water like a camel in the bathrooms, trying to get my blood alcohol level down. There I was, deep-throating the tap, drinking the tame warm water of that tame city Zaragoza. I swear it did so little to bring the level down that it wasn't worth it to turn my belly into a swamp, to give up wine.

Authority destroys us. It is not life or excess or shouting or the

88

savage nocturnal nature of my pain that destroys me. It is authority that destroys me.

There was a kid next to me, twenty-six years old. The kid was in despair: he hadn't even paid off the first instalment of the car. He called his mother. His mother burst into tears. The police dealt with him without any compassion. Not me. I cared about this kid. I cared about his mother. I cared about him. I saw myself in him, all those years ago. I know what it is to be poor and to try to stop being poor. We are all poor. My father was poor. My grandfather was poor. 'I earn a thousand euros a month, and the car costs me four hundred, and now these guys are taking six hundred as a fine,' the guy said and his mother cried. 'Nice round number,' one of the constables said. And then he added, 'Shouldn't have drunk so much.' Well, in this instance he was right, the constable, because the kid said to me when the two of us were left alone: *But I only had five whiskies, and yes, I know I should have had them with a bit of ice, like my girlfriend says, but you know, it's just, look, I like them like that, straight up, nothing extra, down the hatch. We're going to get married next year, me and my girlfriend, we've got a flat picked out and everything, we were going to go and look at bedroom furniture tomorrow, pine, from Ikea, all very cheap, a good thing she went home before all this.*

I said goodbye to the pigs, who were eating overripe oranges, tinned tuna, soft doughnuts and out-of-date satsumas, all of that piled up on the table, next to their hats and the alcohol-measuring kit.

The sun was already shining on the world, warming the wretched windows of that police station on the outskirts of the city of Zaragoza.

Warm my soul, sun, I conceive you.

I saw a workers' bar, and went in and ordered a gin and tonic with stale ice-cubes in a chipped glass. I had my MP3 player in the pocket of my coat and put on The Who. Just imagine: eight-thirty in the morning with 'The Kids Are Alright' sounding in my head, and me, almost absent from the bar, trying to be happy, remembering the monkeys up in their trees. I can't complain, I'm still alive. I'm alive, and there's no way they can kill me, I'm one lucky guy. I remember the man I was. I'm alive, and I ordered another gin and tonic, and it was nine-thirty. And the light seemed the greatest and most terrible space in my heart, dogs biting it all. Wonderful, all of it wonderful.

From the bar, I saw the kid and his mother leaving the police station. They walked out holding one another. They were like lovers. I didn't hear anything, just The Who. I was drunk again, they could have given me another breathalyser. It would have been fun. Here I am again, measure my wickedness once again, my innocence, my desire to live, measure it all. Measure the alcohol in my blood. Hey, here I am again, with even more alcohol this time. I don't want this intensity to fade ever again, if it fades then I'll die. And I don't want to die, not ever. If it fades I will die: I can't die, I just can't, don't you get it? It's impossible for me to die. If this dies, this, this and this, what will become of life? Oceans and deserts and the hard rocks of the world never die, like I, who am neither an ocean nor a desert nor a world. What am I? I think I am love. Wonderful. I thought that my poetry was imperfect, and that life within me had been so as well. But my poetry is in the service of life. Life is great. Wonderful. More, I want more. A thousand times more of everything. Wonderful.

The world is poison, and the world gives me earthly life. The world is fire in my mouth. I believe in the world,. I believe in you all. Rise up. Burn it all. Don't take too long. I'd like to see it. Wonderful.

Walk on the Wild Side

(Iraq, April 2003)

The sergeant looks out through a huge window
at the desert's empty eye sockets, the infantry cranes
like hydraulic palm trees sprouting from the sandy hills,
the mule carts, a lost goat with a hole in its side
surrounded by hair and blood,
a steaming dog,
a broken-down car that is steaming too, an '86 Fiat,
the sun hurling itself lovelessly on the wonderful dungheaps,
the whole great day of it.
A great and needful day, a fleshy slap in the face.
And he looks down at his black skin for a while, blending with all
    the other skins.

The American sergeant
goes into one of Saddam's palaces, breaking
the door with a hefty kick –
the kind that Rubén Darío would have given,
that old Indian, poor and dirty,
whom I read so much and loved so much in vain,
in vain, in vain, in vain,
yes, we are talking about America –
he sits down in one of the luxurious armchairs,
hums a Bob Dylan song
and then dances a little and moves with grace and is happy
and smokes a good cigar and tells the corporal a joke.

The corporal relieves himself against one of the walls,
underneath a portrait of Saddam,
and laughs a lot at how badly the sergeant sings;
if he could he'd put a bullet through his brain,
that dry Arizona brain –
they're quite drunk, bored and drunk,
but happy,
. drinking cold beer all morning and eating peanuts
manufactured in China for the United States Army,

unleashing the fury of their molars
on warm imported peanuts,
pressing their teeth together, breaking China apart.

This too is democracy, oh my brother:
an African-American (the sergeant)
and a half-black Hispanic (the corporal)
walking into the most exclusive palaces of the Orient.

The sergeant calls his girlfriend from his mobile and whispers
oh, baby, this is better than fucking you.
You're drunk, you fucking son of a bitch, she whispers back,
I'm screwing your brother right as we speak.
Make sure you suck his dick like he deserves, the sergeant says.

And then the lieutenant, the sergeant and the corporal go off
with three Iraqi sluts, if any are still left alive.

The colonel doesn't go out fucking because his wife is a senator.
The Senator from Montana, *try screwing her*. I'm sick of screwing
      her, to be honest.

The lieutenant gets first pick,
and he picks the one who looks least like Frankenstein's monster.
The hookers walk with terror into the Republican suites,
for they still remember.
This bed, this whole room is yours, the black sergeant
says to one of the women. *All yours, here you go, take this fucking lamp*
and he reaches his dark hands to the oil-lamp on the bedside table.

Women always lose two wars, or three wars, or a million wars.

The sergeant gives one Iraqi a kick up the ass
when he finds she has only four fingers on her right hand.
You're missing a finger, you fucking witch,
trying to trick me.

He leaves his pistol on the bedside table.

The black sergeant hums *Blowin' In The Wind*.

Hey man, the world makes you laugh, doesn't it.

'Here, take a photo,' and they take a photo.

Here they are, the three of them: the sergeant, the lieutenant and
    the corporal.
Baghdad, April 2003.
Five million megapixels.
Walk On The Wild Side, that should be the title.

Maybe they start going to see a shrink in 2006,
and lose their hair in 2008, and are drunk all day by 2010,
and in 2013 they all turn into black men,
and in 2015 they are cheap and absurd women,
and in 2016 they embrace Islam, but monstrously and way too hard,
and in 2017 they are shadow-ghosts in the Brooklyn parks,
and in 2018 they throw themselves into the Hudson,
to swim a little among the gasoline, the corruption, the seaweed,
the skulls, the theatres, the nothingness, the light and their famous
    lack of guilt,
the most famous light of guiltlessness that grows like the moon,
the exhausting light of all times
in which we were unhappy and impermanent, snakes, shining snakes
that touch history with a sweet cheapness,
that turns me on till I am bright, bright, bright.

Shame I couldn't have come with you, men,
I sure like them hookers.

Our Air

(the first few summers of the 21st century)

Spain: air-conditioning units (Carrier, Samsung, Sharp, Roca, Hitachi, Fujitsu) hanging from thousands of windows, hospitals with huge cold air machines, and the extractor tubes making the air wretched, the dying sun up there, and after the heat, the ridiculous storms, gales filled with hailstones and lightning.

Tramps standing in the public fountains, their black feet next to the gold fish, the fish already old, the last of their tribe, hot and desperate, seeking a foot against which to shipwreck themselves and die, to die biting human flesh, the flesh of the people responsible for all this.

And the sun with its coronas crowned with waste and crystallised thought, and the clouds fleeing, and the great white sharks sinking to the depths to die in the darkness, and then there'll be a cold autumn and a warm winter. And in Paris people get on it too, running out of supermarkets with air-conditioning units – goodbye to their old-fashioned rotary fans – and in London, girls who are six foot tall, red-haired with freckles, have discovered how to use fans, and girls in Oslo sweat right through their underwear.

The world is heating up.

Avenues in Spanish cities at three o'clock in the afternoon on 3 August at forty-three degrees in the shade, and flats and traffic lights turning to smoke, the acceleration of subatomic particles.

The furniture we inherited from our grandmother starts suddenly to burn on 3 August at three o'clock in the afternoon at forty-three degrees in the shade, our air.

The suburban bars with next-generation air-conditioning units with remote controls. And Mercedes with their windows rolled right up, and Renaults as well. And the sea, a sewer. Our air. The North Pole is warming, and it melts, in love and burnt.

We will burn.

The warm water in the swimming pools.

The inhuman swerve of the sun above our soft, ardent foreheads.

The rubber evaporating from the car tyres.

No desire for anything.

Solid boredom.

Heat is winning the battle.

Our air.

And the dogs with their tongues out, the desiccated birds in the trees, the trees trying to move to find some kind of shade, the yellow flowers, the cloud of rubbish that keeps on mounting, the universal waste-tip.

And everything is like that, a huge bluish flare-up, the earth cut into chunks like a King-Kong-sized cow in an abattoir.

Six billion people in the world's bonfire, breathing our air. Six billion people warming their blood with the blood of the planet.

Don't tell me that you haven't yet got a Carrier. Disgusting sweat all hours of the day. Desire to sweat. Don't tell me you still only have a fan, a Taurus, or one of those ceiling fans, monotonous, colonial, Francoist, Stalinist, Victorian, Goalist, Vilasist. Because when Carrier touches our grotesque air, it turns it into a fresh breeze, a wet kiss, and then, only then can I finish this poem.

Oh, sweet Carrier, it's my wife and it's my life.

I have loved it all, all of it.

Now I can die in peace.

I burnt my lips loving it all, really, I was in love with it all and I still am, our air.

Let me die in peace, like a mountain dog, a good boy, probably.

Oh, sweet Carrier, it's my wife and it's my life.

I'm not going to be with you one minute more. I am sick of you kicking me. I said, you kick me. And I'm sick of your shirts, of washing them and ironing them. Your shirts are disgusting, so ugly, and I was the one who picked them out. I don't love you, do you hear me, I don't love you. I don't love football or tennis or novels about Romans or aliens or dragons or Oriental chests or whatever it is that you read at night before you go to sleep like a pig. You hear me? I don't like football, not at all, not a tiny, tiny bit. I think it's gross, football. I don't like your mother, or your sister, or your cousins. Get out. I've been with you for ten years and in ten years I haven't opened my mouth. You don't know how to make coffee. You don't know how to make love. You don't know how to make a tortilla. You don't know how to call the plumber. You don't know how to hang the washing. You don't know how to love me. You don't know how to smile. I feel sorry for you, yes, I feel sorry for you. Sorry. Yes, sorry, because none of this is your fault. Yes, it's true, all you can do is set the alarm clock and then drink a beer with your friends after working for ten hours (and don't worry, I'm not going to fuck your friends, not even if they were the last dildoes on the planet, because they are as monstrous as you are, as guiltlessly monstrous, no more than that). You are a post-industrial Dracula, my love. Working for ten hours. I've spent ten years hearing about your ten hours. Ten years of ten hours a day and all for nothing. 'My job's so important,' you say. Oh yes, you can really see how your work's changing the world. A little different every day, the world is, with you putting the hours in. Go on, set the alarm clock. Your shirt's already ironed for tomorrow. You'll have a lot of work tomorrow, my love. Poor little thing, love of my life. Go on, go to bed. Poor little thing, you'll not find anyone now, you don't even have the guts to get a lover. My stupid husband wouldn't know what to do with a lover. Yes, I know you're earning lots of money, and we'll buy new furniture and get a new car. Great. Marvellous. I could fuck the plumber, the policeman who brings the parking tickets because you don't know how to park, our neighbour from the fifth floor, the sixth floor, the third floor, and you wouldn't ever notice a thing. You'd never notice anything. A proper wood table and a Renault Mégane and a week in Cancún. Your checked shirt, your belt, your Tergal trousers, your moccasins. Go on, my love, I'll set the alarm clock, you'll have to do the same tomorrow as you did today, great isn't it. Work, my love, get up early, my love. Your only sybaritic touch, a bottle of Loewe cologne from the duty free. And please die soon, my love. I'd like to see you die, that would really turn me on, that would open my slit from Ibiza to the Norfolk Broads. Die soon, you piece of shit, you ruin my life every moment you're alive, every moment.

The Kids Are Alright

(5 January 2007)

On 5 January I went to Barcelona, from Barbastro, where I was
freezing my tits off. In Barcelona it was not only not cold, but I even
had a dip at the Barceloneta beach, where it was 17 degrees at one
p.m. I adore Barcelona. I like its light, and it's always warm there.
A black kid was bathing alongside me. Whenever I do anything
memorable I look around and there's a black kid or a Chinese kid.
We laughed together in the waves. I'd forgotten my swimming
trunks. Neither of us was cold. Neither of us had swimming trunks.
Naked in the waves, swimming and forgetting about the cold. Then
I had rice with lobster and drank a bottle of Miserere, and went to
buy CDs of The Who, which is what I like to do most of all: buy
CDs and DVDs and books about The Who and buy them all. All
the versions you can get of 'The Kids Are Alright', always that song.
Barcelona was like Fifth Avenue. Two hundred kilometres from
Fifth Avenue there are villages in Aragón that are filled with fog,
filled with nothing and nobody. What a contrast. How wild. Spain
is like that, but what can I care about it, because I'm alright, yes, I'm
OK. I was always innocent. I myself am innocence. I'm lucky. My
kids are lucky. My kids are blessed. My black kids are alright, they
eat and make love every day and don't vote every four years because
they don't believe in it. They breathe and live and die and that's all.
2007 is good, right, it's going alright. If you want to dance with
my girl, then I don't care. Keep her. Have children with her, get
married, build a home, a family, be blessed. Why should I care if
you're making love to my girl if she's happy and you're alright? No
problem with that. I don't want there to be laws. My Chinese kids
are alright too. They work hard and smile for no reason. They ride
their red motorbikes all round the city, with egg-fried rice in plastic
pots. They earn nothing, a pittance, but they're alright because life is
like that. Life is good. Life was always OK. I like those motorbikes,
all the noise they make. I like expensive red wine, like the song says.
Well, this is how I want to wish you a happy 2007. I want to kiss
you. I want to meet up with you at three in the afternoon, very
early, and walk with you until six in the morning, very late. I want
to marry you, and I want all these kids to come to the wedding,

because these kids are alright. I still haven't gone. It's 2007 and I still haven't gone. I'm not going to go. I don't think I'm ever going to die, no, not ever. I look at my kids, and they're alright. The bells are ringing, there must be a party somewhere. After drinking and dancing, let's go for a swim and watch the sun come up. We'll swim very far out to sea, and we won't drown, because we're alright, the kids are alright. I can't miss a single party. Don't give my kids jobs that make them despair, don't bring them down. Don't give my kids ballot boxes with your name already inside them. Don't mess with my kids, because all the bells of the future are ringing.

The Crematorium

I asked these two guys where the oven was,
it was the night of 18 December 2005,
down the Monzón road (*don't you know where Monzón is?*
It's a village lost in the desert).
Storms up in the mountains, and over the nothingness, naked
as a brand-new bride, the low-slung moon of dead highways.
Monzón, Barbastro, my eternal stomping grounds.
They let me look through the little window and there was the
    coffin burning,
cracking, the coffin already red hot.

The thermometer showed eight hundred degrees.
I imagined what my father must be like in the box.
And the box in the fire and my heart in the terror.
I was even losing my desire to hate.
Desire that had kept me alive all these years.
And my desire to love, what became of that? Do you know that,
oh Lord of the great deaths who drives
your political prisoners to churning hunger, to durability,
to an eternity of being unsatisfied, oh, you bastard –
You pluck me out –
love of God, oh, you bastard?

Pick up this man in the middle of the desert.
Or don't pick him up, how could I possibly care
for your icy presence in this drunken night
that has been and will be either against you or in your favour,
it's all the same, how wonderful, it's all the same.
The end and the beginning, all the same, how wonderful.
Love and hate, the same; kisses and buttocks,
all the same; wondrous coition at the heart of one's youth
and the putrefaction and decrepitude of the flesh,
all the same, how wonderful.

The oven runs on diesel, the man said.
And we looked up at the chimney,
and because it was night,

the flames hit out
against the cold December sky,
the wastelands of Monzón,
by Barbastro, freezing in the fields,
three degrees below zero,
those fields of witches and vampires and people such as I;
'It all goes up there,' the man said,
a calm, obese man,
underdressed for the cold,
his belly almost open to the air,
'It takes two or three hours, depending on how much the deceased
    weighs,
he said deceased, but he was thinking sausage or sack of shit,
once we burnt a gentleman who weighed one hundred and twenty
    kilos,
and it took quite a while,' he said.
'A very large gentleman, I think,' he added.

'My father only weighed seventy kilos,' I said.
'Well, then it will take much less time,'
the man said. The coffin was now little bits of air or smoke.
The next day me and my brother came back
and they gave us the urn, we had chosen a cheap urn,
you can get urns that cost as much as six thousand euros,
the man had said.

'This is all we are,' the man said in a ritual fashion,
wanting to become a human being, although
neither he nor we knew what a human being is,
and he gave me the urn inside a blue plastic bag.
And I thought about him, how fat he was, how long he would take
to burn in his own oven. And as if he had heard me
he said, 'Much longer than your father,' and gave a bitter smile.

Then I said, 'The one who will take an eternity
to burn is me, because my heart
is solid rock, and my flesh wild iron
and my soul a volcano
of blood at three million degrees,

and I would break your oven just by touching it,
believe me, I would put you out of business,
better I don't die anywhere near here.'
Anywhere near here, the wastelands of Monzón,
B roads,
Barbastro in the distance, lit very badly,
and by now four degrees below zero.

Take your father's ashes and get out of here.

Yes, I'm going, I wish I could burn like my father
burned, I wish that it could burn,
this hand or tongue or liver of God
that I have inside of me,
this life of inextinguishable
and irredeemable conscience;
the extinction of good and evil,
which are the same in Him.
The non-extinction of all that I am.

I wish his eight-hundred-degree oven could burn all that I am.
Burn flesh at a thousand million inhuman degrees.
I wish there was a fire that could extinguish all that I am.
Because it doesn't matter if what I am is good or bad.
Extinguish, extinguish, extinguish all I am; that would be Glory.

Take your father's ashes and get out of here.
Don't show your face round here again, I'm telling you, I'll pray
for your father. Your father was a good man
and I don't know who you are, don't show your face round here
    again,
I'm telling you. Please, don't look at me, please.

I had a white Seat 124, I went to Lérida,
I met the tailors of Lérida and of Teruel,
I ate with other tailors in Zaragoza,
but now there are no tailors anywhere,
a voice said.

I am so alone now, dad.
Dad, what am I going to do now.
If I can't see you again I can't see anything.
Where are you, are you with the Lord?
I am so alone here, here on earth.
I am so alone, dad.
Don't make me laugh, you dickhead.
Oh, you son of a bitch, you've been with me,
wherever I was, without leaving the flames.
I've travelled a lot this year, a huge amount.
In all the cities of the earth, in its memorable hotels,
in its dirty and unmemorable hotels as well,
in all the streets, the boats and the planes,
in my laughter, you were there, as round
as an eternal memory, ecumenical and luminous,
round as mercy, compassion and joy,
round as the sun and the moon,
round as glory, as power, round as life.

Communion Rail

It may be that you're not that familiar with the outskirts of Zaragoza,
an ambiguous, frontier world, mysterious.
Outskirts are not the same as suburbs.
They are a slow war waged between brick and earth,
between asphalt and untilled land,
between streetlamps and the moon.
Between the living and the dead.
Between saints and sinners.
Between gladiators and Christians.

Beyond Torrero, beyond Actur,
out there where the emanations of the supermarket no longer reach,
beyond Las Fuentes,
there's a world of asphalted ghost streets
that lead to orchards with no trees
and irrigation cuts with no water,
of bars next to desperate rubble,
a world that leaves you feeling blind;
desolate bars, country huts
next to recently erected cranes,
a world of sad bricklayers who talk Romanian,
who transform
into mad luminescent vampires with very cheap batteries,
all is cheap in this my kingdom,
a world of tortured tyres,
of little shops that sell mass-produced bread
and hot sweet pastries.

The outskirts are also a kingdom of youth:
this is where the future lies for thirty-year-olds,
their flat and their long-term debt to the old men.
The old men have power and nothingness,
they own the laws and the money and the old women, whom
they no longer fuck – this is all an unending lie –
and they are the owners of the roofs, the walls,
the domestication of this cold land,
its sticky coldness.

It is out here that the young can expect golden Sundays to enjoy
their nineteen-square-metre sitting room,
their seven-square-metre kitchen, their ten-square-metre
    'dormitory-suite' –
which is what the constructor called it the day they signed the
    contract –
their garage spot that will protect their '87 Corsa
from the barbarous wind of the recently levelled ground,
their wonderful views of the motorway leading to Barcelona.
Look at those views, honey,
look at the way the sun burns in our faces,
look at how we will end up like them,
like the guys who sold us this shit,
how we will be rednecks, cheap souls,
so let me do everything to you tonight,
the only night we have. Let me eat
what they do not have: your sweet white flesh
and let me permanently satisfy
your glorious desire to fuck. This is our kingdom.

When insomnia arrives, and it will arrive, then count,
my love, so as not to go mad, count the cars
that drive past
at two hundred kilometres per hour
(with sophisticated equipment
to detect the radar guns
used by the cheap Spanish police authorities)
in the depths of a night that is as insignificant
as the hot sweet pastries they sell in the shop on the corner.

My love don't quit your job, my love
if you want we can fuck until we die, but please
don't quit your job.